# KNOW YOUR RIGHTS!

## FOURTH EDITION

Richard M. Alderman
"The People's Lawyer"

# KNOW YOUR RIGHTS!

## FOURTH EDITION

Answers to Texans'
Everyday Legal Questions

**Gulf Publishing Company**
**Houston, Texas**

# KNOW YOUR RIGHTS!

## FOURTH EDITION

10   9   8   7   6   5   4   3   2   1

**Library of Congress Cataloging-in-Publication Data**

Alderman, Richard M.
    Know your rights! : answers to Texans' everyday legal
questions / Richard M. Alderman. — 4th ed.
      p.  cm.
    ISBN 0-88415-419-X
    1. Law—Texas—Popular works.   I. Title.
KFT1281.A37 1994
349.764—dc20
[347.64]                                   94-15666
                                         CIP

*This publication is designed to provide accurate and
authoritative information with regard to the subject matter
covered. It is sold with the understanding that neither the
publisher nor the author is engaged in rendering legal advice
to specific individuals.*

*IF LEGAL SERVICE OR OTHER EXPERT ASSISTANCE
IS REQUIRED, THE SERVICES OF A COMPETENT
PROFESSIONAL SHOULD BE SOUGHT.*

*To my grandparents*

# CONTENTS

CHAPTER EIGHT

# Door-to-Door Sales ............................ 77

CHAPTER NINE

# Employment ................................. 80

CHAPTER TEN

# False & Deceptive Acts ......................... 87

# PREFACE TO THE FIRST EDITION

You may not think about it, but nearly every day *you* have to know the law. Not only lawyers must make decisions based on knowledge of the law, but people like yourself must apply basic legal principles in daily life. And if you do not know the law, you are making decisions partially uninformed.

The Texas and federal legislatures have passed scores of laws designed to protect you in your everyday transactions. Most of these laws are considered self-regulating. This means that the laws are supposed to work because you know about them, and your knowledge keeps merchants from trying to violate the laws. The breakdown in this system is apparent: Because most people do not know their legal rights, the laws often do not work.

This book is designed to ensure that our laws do work by helping you learn about them. The book covers a wide variety of topics ranging from credit-card rights, to landlord-tenant relations, to the legal aspects of warranties and wills. The choice of topics and the format of the book are based on my personal experience as "The People's Lawyer" for a Houston television station.

As the People's Lawyer, I have received thousands of letters about the most common legal problems. This mail has led me to two conclusions: First, many of you share the same everyday legal problems to which you do not know the answers; and second, there is no readily available source of information. This book was written to address both problems.

But this book is not designed to make you a lawyer, nor is it meant to encourage lawsuits. Instead, it is designed to make you aware of the choices and rights you have under the law. Whether you are dealing with a store that will not replace a damaged television set, a neighbor whose barking dog keeps you awake all night, or, perhaps, a landlord who deducts too much from your security deposit, you must know your legal rights in order to reach a fair and equitable solution.

Once *someone* knows *you* know your rights, he is usually quick to try to work something out. Compromise and settlement—not litigation—should be the goal of any legal system. It is the goal of this book.

*Richard M. Alderman*

# PREFACE TO THE FOURTH EDITION

As I noted in the original preface to this book, my goal in writing *Know Your Rights!* was to help everyday people understand the law, enabling them to better stand up for their rights. The book has been even more successful than I imagined. Now, eight years after its initial publication, I find I must, for the third time, add to the book to keep up with the increasing number of legal questions I have received and the changes made by the courts and legislature.

The format of this edition remains the same. What has changed is the coverage. In the first edition, I discussed what I believed to be the most common legal questions people have. In the second and third editions, I added several new chapters and expanded many of the existing ones. For example, divorce, immigration law, and employment were all added. In this edition, I have expanded the coverage of nearly every chapter and have updated the answers to comply with current law.

Also, as you might expect, some of the material in the earlier editions has become out of date or incorrect because of action by the courts and legislature. A problem with any book on law is keeping it current. With the publication of this edition you now have the most up-to-date information available. It is unavoidable, however, that even this edition is dated. The material is based on the law as it existed as of May 1994.

Those of you who are buying this book to replace your third edition already know how invaluable a resource it can be. If this is your first purchase, let me just emphasize what I said in the first edition. *Once someone knows that you know your legal rights, he is usually quick to try to work something out.* I hope that you find this book is one of the best investments you have ever made.

*Richard M. Alderman*

# CHAPTER ONE

# Applying for Credit

FOR most of us, credit is an essential part of life. Our homes, our cars, and much of our personal property are all purchased on credit. Just imagine what it would be like if we had to pay for everything with cash. Yes, America is truly a land of consumer credit; together we owe hundreds of billions of dollars.

Because of the importance of obtaining credit, Congress has passed three laws to protect people who are trying to get it:

First:

**The Equal Credit Opportunity Act** ensures that all credit applicants start off on the same foot by prohibiting discrimination based on color, age, sex, race, or marital status.

Second:

**The Truth-in-Lending Law** protects individuals from paying "too much" for credit by requiring that all relevant information be disclosed before a contract is signed and, more importantly, that the information be provided in an understandable manner. (In other words, you *must* be given enough information to permit you to shop around for credit.)

Third:

**The Fair Credit Reporting Act** requires that you have a full opportunity to find out what information is in your credit report. It also gives you the right to correct any errors that might exist in that information.

When you apply for credit, you should know the law. You should also know what factors are important in obtaining credit, and what information your creditors "cannot" use to deny you credit. As you will discover in the following letters, there are legal solutions for some of the more common problems you may experience while trying to obtain credit.

## Why can't I get credit?
## "You must be told why."

*Dear Mr. Alderman:*
*I need your help. I can't figure out why no one will give me credit. I have applied for two credit cards and, both times, I was turned down. I have a good job and I have never had financial problems. What can I do to get credit?*

If you have been turned down for credit and have not been told why, someone has violated the law. Under the Equal Credit Opportunity Act, you must be notified of the decision within 30 days after your application was completed. *If credit is denied, you must be notified in writing. The notification must explain the specific reasons for the denial or inform you that you may request a full explanation.*

If you are denied credit, be sure to find out why. In your case, reread the letter you received and see if it tells you whom to contact for an explanation. If it does not, write the creditor and demand that he explain the specific reasons for denying you credit. You should also consider contacting the Federal Trade Commission to report that the creditor is not complying with the law. The FTC has a regional office in Dallas:

Federal Trade Commission
100 N. Central Expy.
Suite 500
Dallas, TX 75201

After you find out why you were denied credit, you can take steps to correct the problem. It may be that the creditor thinks you have asked for too much money, or that you have not been employed or lived in the community long enough. Once you know why, you can discuss these reasons with the creditor and attempt to work it out. Sometimes you will discover that the creditor simply had incorrect information. As you will see in the next letter, credit reports may be wrong, and when they are, you can correct them.

## How do I get a copy of my credit report?
## "A new law may help."

*Dear Mr. Alderman:*
*I have had problems getting credit because of prior debt problems. I have had a good credit history for the past eight years, and I now*

*want to make sure that my credit report is accurate and that the neg-
ative information has been removed. How do I go about getting a
copy of my report?*

Under a new Texas law, a credit bureau must provide you with a copy
of all information contained in its file concerning you. The copy must be
provided within 45 days of your request.

I suggest you immediately call the credit bureau and request a copy of
your file. They may ask for some identification information to insure that
you are the person you claim to be. Under prior law, they also were
allowed to charge you a small fee unless you had been turned down for
credit within the past 30 days. As I understand the new law, the report
must be provided at no charge.

If you find there are any inaccuracies in the report, you can take steps
to have them corrected. The next letter explains how to do this.

### What can I do if my credit report is wrong?
### "You have rights."

*Dear Mr. Alderman:*
*I was just refused a credit card. I was told the reason was that I had
missed several payments on my motor home . . . but I don't even own a
motor home. When I asked where they obtained this information, they
said it was in my credit report. What should I do? I am sure all my
creditors believe I am living in a motor home that I'm not paying for.*

There is a law that protects you from having inaccurate information in
your credit report. It is the Fair Credit Reporting Act. This law protects
you from inaccurate reporting of credit information by giving you the
right to find out what is in your report, and allowing you to require that
the reporting agency correct any errors. Because of the importance of
having an accurate and up-to-date credit file, I suggest you contact the
credit reporting agency immediately and assert your rights under this law.

The Fair Credit Reporting Act applies to any "consumer reporting
agency." The most common type of consumer reporting agency is the
credit bureau. Information gathered by a credit bureau, called a "consumer report," is sold to creditors, employers, insurance companies, and
other businesses for the purpose of evaluating your credit-worthiness. If
you are denied credit due to information contained in such a report, the
creditor must give you the name and address of the credit reporting

agency. I assume that in your case, the creditor supplied you with this information.

The next step is to contact the credit reporting agency and request a full report of the information in your file. Under a new Texas law, the agency must provide you with a copy of the report within 45 days. If you have been denied credit, you must be given a copy at no charge. The law is unclear as to whether a charge may be imposed in other cases. In my opinion, however, a charge may not be imposed.

Under the law, the credit reporting agency must tell you about every piece of information it has concerning you. You also must be told the names of everyone who has been given a copy of the report within the past six months.

If you disagree with any of the information, you have the right to demand that the agency reinvestigate the items in question. If the new investigation reveals an error, the agency must send a corrected version of the report to everyone who received the old report within the past six months.

In your case, demand that the credit bureau reinvestigate. If the credit bureau discovers you do not own a motor home, it must renotify your creditors and give them a copy of the accurate report. Sometimes, though, the credit bureau will stand by its original report.

For example, a creditor may have reported that a consumer was late in paying some bills. The consumer was paying late only because the bills were not sent on time. The credit bureau may refuse to change the report because the creditor still says the consumer was late. If this happens, you have the right to include a brief statement containing your version of why you were late. This statement will become part of your file and will be sent out whenever a creditor requests a credit report.

You should also be aware that there is a time limit on how long credit information can be reported by a consumer-reporting agency. Generally, after seven years, information is considered obsolete and may not be reported. There are, however, a few exceptions to this rule:

- Bankruptcy information can be reported for up to 10 years.
- No time limit exists for information reported for a prospective job with a salary of more than $20,000.
- No time limit exists for information reported on more than $50,000 worth of credit or life insurance.

If you have ever applied for a charge account, a personal loan, insurance, or a job, someone probably has a file on you. This file might contain any information that creditors use to determine your credit-worthiness. Everything, including how quickly you pay your bills, whether you have ever filed bankruptcy, or whether you have ever been sued, may be written into your credit report.

Because a good credit report is so important, it would be a good idea to check your file *before* a problem arises. It is quite easy to call your nearest credit bureau (see list below) and arrange for an interview.

### Amarillo
Amarillo Credit Association, 912 S. Taylor St., P.O. Box 470, Amarillo, TX 79184; telephone (806) 374-1611 and 374-3758.

### Austin
Merchants and Professional Credit Bureau, P.O. Box 140675, Austin, TX 78714; telephone (512) 346-4305.

### Beaumont
Credit Bureau of Greater Beaumont, 3830 Highway 365, Port Arthur, TX 77642; telephone (409) 721-8701.

### Corpus Christi
Credit Bureau of Corpus Christi, 4444 Corona Dr., Suite 135, Corpus Christi, TX 78411; telephone (210) 686-8293

### Dallas
CSC Credit Services, 250 E. Arapaho Rd., #126, Richardson, TX 75081; telephone (214) 669-9029.

### East Texas
CSC Credit Services, 300 East Main, Suite 300, P.O. Box 630950, Nacogdoches, TX 75963; telephone (409) 564-7341.

### El Paso
CSC Credit Services, 4120 Rio Bravo, Suite 319, El Paso, TX 79902; telephone (915) 779-6153.

### Houston
CSC Credit Services, 2100 Travis St., Suite 320, P.O. Box 674402, Houston, TX 77267; telephone (713) 878-1990.

### Laredo
Credit Bureau of Laredo, Inc. See Corpus Christi.

### McAllen
CSC Credit Services. See Corpus Christi.

### Midland-Odessa
Credit Data, P.O. Box 60635, Midland, TX 79711; telephone (915) 536-5136.

**San Antonio**
 Associated Credit Services, Inc., 84 N.E. Loop 410, Suite 124, San
 Antonio, TX 78216; telephone (210) 525-1171.
**South Central Texas**
 See San Antonio.
**Victoria**
 Credit Bureau of Victoria, 2001 E. Sabine, Suite 206, Victoria, TX
 77901; telephone (512) 573-9161.

### How can my ex-spouse's debts appear on my credit report?
### "They were your debts as well."

*Dear Mr. Alderman:*
*My former common law husband and I bought a car and financed it*
*through his credit union. He was the buyer. I just co-signed the note.*
*After he missed two payments, they repossessed the car. They asked*
*me to pay but I told them that as far as I was concerned this was his*
*debt. Now they have put this on my credit report. Can they do this?*

Basically the answer is yes. As I discuss on page 36, co-signing a note is
a very serious undertaking. You are agreeing to the same obligation as the
other person. If he doesn't pay, you have to. If there is a default, it is your
default as well. The information will appear on both your credit reports.

 Remember, you have the right to add your own statement to your credit report explaining information contained in it. You may want to add a
brief statement indicating that this was your husband's debt.

### How can I shop for credit?
### "Truth-in-Lending."

*Dear Mr. Alderman:*
*I am in the market for a new car. I know it's important to get the best*
*interest rate, but it is all so confusing. There are all kinds of ads with*
*different rates, and every time I call to ask about interest, they tell*
*me about the APR. What is an APR? How can I compare interest*
*rates as well as price? It seems that you can't find out the interest*
*rate until after you buy something.*

Until recently creditors were free to confuse consumers by using all
sorts of language when they loaned you money. Interest rates could be

*(text continued on page 8)*

**A credit sales contract should be written in standard language and should clearly reveal all costs involved in the transaction.**

**Big Wheel Auto**                                          Alice Green

| ANNUAL PERCENTAGE RATE The cost of your credit as a yearly rate. | FINANCE CHARGE The dollar amount the credit will cost you. | Amount Financed The amount of credit provided to you or on your behalf | Total of Payments The amount you will have paid after you have made all payments as scheduled | Total Sale Price The total cost of your purchase on credit, including your downpayment of $ _1500 -_ |
|---|---|---|---|---|
| 14.84 % | $1496.80 | $6107.50 | $7604.30 | $9129.30 |

You have the right to receive at this time an itemization of the Amount Financed.
☐ I want an itemization.   ☒ I do not want an itemization.

Your payment schedule will be:

| Number of Payments | Amount of Payments | When Payments Are Due |
|---|---|---|
| 36 | $211.23 | Monthly beginning 6-1-94 |

**Insurance**
Credit life insurance and credit disability insurance are not required to obtain credit, and will not be provided unless you sign and agree to pay the additional cost.

| Type | Premium | Signature | |
|---|---|---|---|
| Credit Life | $120 - | I want credit life insurance. | alice Green   Signature |
| Credit Disability | | I want credit disability insurance. | Signature |
| Credit Life and Disability | | I want credit life and disability insurance. | Signature |

**Security:** You are giving a security interest in:
☒ the goods being purchased.
☐ _____

Filing fees $ _12.50_          Non-filing insurance $ _____

**Late Charge:** If a payment is late, you will be charged $10.

**Prepayment:** If you pay off early, you
☐ may  ☐ will not   have to pay a penalty.
☒ may  ☐ will not   be entitled to a refund of part of the finance charge.

See your contract documents for any additional information about nonpayment, default, any required repayment in full before the scheduled date, and prepayment refunds and penalties.

I have received a copy of this statement.
_alice Green_          _5-1-94_
Signature                      Date

_____
e means an estimate

*(text continued from page 6)*

quoted as "add on," "discount," or "simple." Terms of an agreement, such as down payment, total price, and penalties, could be hidden throughout the contract, and it would take a lawyer to figure them all out.

But under a law known as "Truth-in-Lending," all this has changed. Under this federal law, creditors must use standard language to disclose terms and must let you see a completed copy of the contract before you sign. *The purpose of Truth-in-Lending is to let you compare rates and shop around.*

On the previous page is a sample credit sales contract. Under the law, if you went to three different car dealers, they would each have to use a substantially similar form so that you would be able to compare how much you would pay and at what interest rate.

*Under the law, interest rates must be disclosed as an annual percentage rate (APR).* This is a mathematical formula that lets you compare rates, no matter how the creditor computes them. Why should you compare? A difference of only a few percentage points in the financing of a car could save you hundreds of dollars.

If you would like a copy of the Truth-in-Lending law, and all of the regulations passed to enforce it, write the Board of Governors of the Federal Reserve System, Washington, DC 20551, and ask for "Regulation Z Truth-in-Lending."

## Are women different?
## "No! Equal credit opportunity exists under the law."

*Dear Mr. Alderman:*

*I am a recently divorced 26-year-old woman. I have been employed for the past five years as the manager of a small baking company, and I think I make a good salary. The other day I went to my bank to borrow some money for a home improvement loan. The bank refused to give me the loan and told me they were afraid a single woman with two children might get married, leave town, and not pay back the loan. Even though I assured them that this would not happen, they insisted I get a co-signer. This doesn't seem fair. I know that one of my male employees who makes less than I do just obtained a loan at this bank. Can they do this?*

It is very difficult to tell if you have been illegally discriminated against, based on your brief letter. There is a law, however, that protects people from credit discrimination. If after reading this you believe that you have been the subject of discrimination, I urge you to contact the appropriate federal agency and file a complaint.

Because of the importance of credit in today's society, Congress has enacted the Equal Credit Opportunity Act. *This law prohibits discrimination against an applicant for credit on the basis of sex, marital status, race, color, religion, national origin, or age.* The law does not ensure that anyone will be given credit, but it does require that the same standard of credit-worthiness be applied to all applicants.

Under the Equal Credit Opportunity Act, a creditor may not turn you down for credit just because you are a woman or single. To protect you from such discrimination the law specifically limits what a creditor may do when you apply for credit:

- A creditor *may not* ask your sex on a credit application—with one exception. If you apply for a loan to buy or build a home, a creditor is *required* to ask your sex to provide the federal government with information to monitor compliance with the act. You do not have to answer the question.

- You *do not* have to choose a courtesy title (Miss, Ms., Mrs.) on a credit form.

- A creditor *may not* request your marital status on an application for an individual, unsecured account (a bank credit card or an overdraft checking account, for example), unless you live in a community property state (Texas *is* a community property state) or rely on property located in a community property state to support your application.

- A creditor *may* request your marital status in all other cases. But, you can only be asked whether you are married, unmarried, or separated (unmarried includes single, divorced, or widowed).

To make sure you are treated fairly once you apply, there are certain things the creditor may not do in deciding whether you are credit-worthy. Specifically, the creditor

- *may not* refuse to consider your income because you are a married woman, even if your income is from part-time employment.

- *may not* ask about your birth control practices or your plans to have children. A creditor may not assume that you will have children or that your income will be interrupted to do so.

- *may not* refuse to consider reliable alimony, child support, or separate maintenance payments. However, you don't have to disclose such income unless you want to in order to improve your chances of getting credit.

- *may not* consider whether you have a telephone listing in your own name, because this would discriminate against married women.
- *may not* consider your sex as a factor in deciding whether you are a good credit risk.
- *may not* use your marital status to discriminate against you.

But there are some closely related questions that are permitted. In order to estimate your expenses, a creditor may ask how many children you have, their ages, and the cost of caring for them (including your obligations to pay alimony, child support, or maintenance). A creditor may ask how regularly you receive your alimony payments or whether they are made under court order, for purposes of determining whether these payments are a dependable source of income. You also may be asked whether there is a telephone in your home.

Finally, a Texas creditor *may* consider your marital status because, under the laws of this state, there may be differences in the property rights of married and unmarried people. Such differences may affect the creditor's ability to collect if you default.

*The law says that a woman has the right to her own credit if she is credit-worthy.* A creditor may not stall you on an application, and he must inform you why credit was denied. If you are not given an explanation, you are entitled to request specific reasons for the denial.

*If you are denied credit, find out why. If you have been discriminated against, the law allows you actual damages plus a penalty. The following agencies are available to assist you if you have been the victim of credit discrimination.*

## Federal Enforcement Agencies

*Retail stores, department stores, consumer finance companies, all other creditors, and all nonbank credit card issuers:*
Federal Trade Commission, Equal Credit Opportunity, Pennsylvania Ave. at Sixth St. NW, Washington, DC 20580, (202) 326-3175.
Regional office: Federal Trade Commission, 100 North Central Expressway, Suite 500, Dallas, TX 75201, (214) 767-5501 (call 8 a.m.–5 p.m., Mon.–Fri.).

*National banks:*
Comptroller of the Currency, Administrator of National Banks, Washington, DC 20219, attn: Consumer Affairs Division, (202) 874-5000.

*State member banks:*
Federal Reserve Bank, 2200 N. Pearl St., Dallas, TX 75201, (214) 922-6000.
Branch banks: Federal Reserve Bank, 1701 San Jacinto, Houston, TX 77002, (713) 659-4433; and Federal Reserve Branch Bank, 126 E. Nueva, P.O. Box 1471, San Antonio, TX 78295, (210) 224-2141.

*Nonmember insured banks:*
Federal Deposit Insurance Corporation, 550 17th St. NW, Washington, DC 20429, (202) 393-8400.
Regional office: Federal Deposit Insurance Corporation, 1910 Pacific Ave., Dallas, TX 75201, (214) 220-3342.

*Savings Institutions insured by the FSLIC and members of the FHLB system (except for savings banks insured by FDIC):*
Office of Thrift Supervision, 1700 G St. NW, Washington, DC 20552, (202) 906-6000.
District office: Federal Home Loan Bank of Dallas, 5605 N. MacArthur, Irving, TX 75038; P.O. Box 619026, Dallas-Fort Worth, TX 75261-9026, (214) 541-8500.

*Creditors subject to Packers and Stockyards Act:*
Office of the Administrator, Packers and Stockyards Administration, Department of Agriculture, Washington, DC 20250-2800, (202) 447-7051.

*Small business investment companies:*
U.S. Small Business Administration, 409 3rd St. SW, Washington, DC 20416, (202) 205-6770.
Hotline number to ask questions: 1-800-827-5722.
Regional office: U.S. Small Business Administration, 8625 King George Drive, Building C, Dallas, TX 75235-3391, (214) 767-7643.
Field offices:
4300 Amon Carter Blvd., Suite 114, Dallas, TX 76155, (817) 885-6500;
Fritz G. Lanham Building, Room 8A32, 819 Taylor, Fort Worth, TX 76102, (817) 334-3613 (score office);
9301 SW Frwy., Suite 550, Houston, TX 77074-1591, (713) 773-6500;
1611 10th St., Suite 200, Lubbock, TX 79401, (806) 743-7462;
10737 Gateway West, Suite 320, El Paso, TX 79935, (915) 540-5676;

222 E. Van Buren St., Suite 500, Harlingen, TX 78550, (210) 427-8533;

606 N. Carancahua, Suite 1200, P.O. Box 9253, Corpus Christi, TX 78476, (512) 888-3301;

North Star Executive Center, 7400 Blanco, Suite 200, San Antonio, TX 78216-4300, (512) 229-4535;

Federal Building, Room 967, 300 E. 8th St., Austin, TX 78701, (512) 482-5288;

*Brokers and Dealers:*

Securities and Exchange Commission, 450 Fifth St., NW, Washington, DC 20549, (202) 272-3100.

Regional office: Securities and Exchange Commission, 801 Cherry St., Suite 1900, Fort Worth, TX 76102, (817) 334-3821.

*Federal Land Banks, Federal Land Bank Associations, Federal Intermediate Credit Banks, and Production Credit Associations:*

Farm Credit Administration, 1501 Farm Credit Drive, McLean, VA 22102-5090, (703) 883-4000.

## What happens when I turn 65?
## "Don't worry."

*Dear Mr. Alderman:*
*I am 64 years young, and I have no intention of retiring. I hope to stay at my present job for at least another 10 years. What I am worried about is that it will become harder for me to get credit, now that I am approaching what many think of as retirement age. I have even heard that some companies will cancel your charge cards if they discover you have reached the age of 65. Is this legal? It shouldn't be; I am just as financially responsible as I ever was.*

The same law that protects the woman in the previous letter from sex discrimination protects you from discrimination based on your age. *The Equal Credit Opportunity Act makes it illegal to discriminate against an applicant for credit based on his or her age.* The law does not prohibit a creditor from considering your age, nor does it guarantee that you will obtain credit. It simply prohibits a creditor from using age as an arbitrary basis for denying or decreasing credit if you otherwise qualify.

In your case, the creditor cannot arbitrarily cancel your credit cards just because you turned 65. This would be a violation of the Equal Credit Opportunity Act. However, if you retired at 65, and your income substantially decreased, this fact could be a sufficient basis for a creditor to deny or limit credit. *The law is clear that a creditor cannot require you to reapply, change the terms of your account, or close your account just because you have reached a certain age.*

I must emphasize, though, that age can be a factor in extension of credit. For example, if you are age 62 and you apply for a 30-year house mortgage, the bank can consider the fact that your retirement income will be less than you presently earn, and that your earning potential is going to decrease. If you were denied the loan based on these considerations, the creditor would not be violating the law.

So how do you determine why you were denied credit? Under the law a creditor must notify you within 30 days of its action and give you specific reasons for its denial, or tell you how to get an explanation. You have the same rights if the creditor closes your account. If, after you receive this information, you think that the real reason was age discrimination, you have the right individually to sue for damages, or you can seek the assistance of a federal agency. There are numerous federal agencies that oversee the Equal Credit Opportunity Act and they are listed earlier in this chapter.

## What about these credit repair services? "Be careful."

*Dear Mr. Alderman:*
*I recently saw an ad for a credit repair service that guaranteed it would fix my bad credit. I called, and they want $500. My credit is so bad that it seems worth it to have it fixed. I just want to make sure that this is all legal. Is it?*

Based on what you said, it may not be. Because of the recent flood of complaints concerning companies offering to "fix" bad credit reports, the Texas Legislature recently enacted a law to try to limit abuse. The new law does not permit payment in advance unless the company has posted a bond. If it has posted a bond, it must give you information about that bond. Credit repair services are not allowed to charge for getting you credit that's available to the general public or misrepresent what they can do. The company also must have available a copy of its registration statement that lists any litigation or unresolved complaints against the company. If you sign a contract for services, you can cancel that contract within three days and get your money back. Finally, any violation of the credit service organization law is also a violation of the Deceptive Trade Practices Act.

*The bottom line:* The Fair Credit Reporting Act, discussed on pages 3 to 6, gives you the right to require that your credit file be accurate. There is no way anyone can have accurate, but negative, information removed from your file. In my opinion, anything the credit repair service can do, you probably can do for yourself for a lot less money.

### Can I be charged more if I use a credit card?
### "Not under Texas law."

*Dear Mr. Alderman:*

*The other day I went shopping for a new microwave oven for my wife. I found one I like but when I went to pay, the store told me that I would have to pay a 5% surcharge if I paid by credit card. The manager told me that because the credit card company charges him a surcharge he was simply passing it on to me. As he explained it, he only gets 95 cents on a dollar from the credit card company, therefore, he has to charge me more to make the same profit. I paid the extra 5% but now I don't think it was right. The store advertises it takes credit cards and it doesn't seem fair that I have to pay more. Is this legal?*

In simple terms . . . no! Texas law says that a merchant may not charge a customer more if he uses a credit card instead of cash. Of course, the law doesn't require that merchants take credit cards, but once they do they may not charge you more. I suggest that you let the store manager know that he didn't have the right to charge you the extra 5%, and that if he doesn't refund it, you will take the store to small claims court. In my opinion, charging this illegal extra amount also violates the Deceptive Trade Practices Act and you could be entitled to three times the extra money you paid. You also may want to let the attorney general's office know about this practice.

### If credit surcharges are illegal, how can a store
### give a discount for cash?
### "They are not the same."

*Dear Mr. Alderman:*
*I don't understand. I heard you on TV and you said that it was ille-*
*gal in Texas to charge more if someone uses a credit card. The next*
*day I went to a gas station and they have two prices, one for cash*
*and one for credit. The credit price was higher. Isn't this illegal?*
*What should I do about it?*

I know this is confusing, but charging more for credit is illegal, while
giving a discount for cash is not. Let me give you an example. Suppose
that a store sells a TV with a list price of $100. If it charged you $104
when you used a credit card, that would be illegal. But if you paid cash,
and only had to pay $96, this discount would be legal, and logical. Here
is why:

When you pay with a credit card, the credit card company does not
give the merchant 100 cents for every dollar you charge. It "discounts"
the amount it pays the merchant. For example, the credit card company
may only give the merchant 96 or 97 cents for every dollar you charge.
*In other words, a merchant pays for the credit when you use a credit*
*card.* By giving you a discount for cash the merchant is simply recogniz-
ing that it saves money when you pay cash and he passes that savings on
to you. That is what the company is doing.

Because the merchant doesn't know who is going to pay cash and who
isn't, the price of any item includes the cost of the credit (the amount the
credit card company will deduct). If a merchant doesn't give you a discount for cash, the merchant is in effect charging you for credit you did-
n't use. As far as I am concerned, every merchant should have two
prices: one cash, one credit. If it doesn't, the cash customers are, in
effect, paying more to subsidize those who use credit. (Of course, the
bottom line, whether you pay cash or credit, is to always shop for the
best price.)

## The credit card company didn't tell me how high
## the interest rate was. Is that legal?
## "No. Not anymore."

*Dear Mr. Alderman:*
*Not too long ago, I got a slick offer in the mail for a new credit card.*
*It guaranteed me a high line of credit and no annual fee. It sounded*
*like too good a deal to pass up, so I signed up. The first month, I*
*paid half my bill, expecting to pay the other half with interest, of*

*course, the following month. I couldn't believe it when the bill arrived. I was charged 24% interest! Is this legal? How come I was never told that in exchange for no annual fee, I was going to be paying a ridiculous interest rate?*

The good news is that what happened to you should never happen again. The bad news is that you probably are stuck with the high interest rate. The best advice I can give you is to cut up the card and shop around for a new one.

Under a law that took effect in August 1989, banks and department stores are required to disclose key financial terms of their credit cards in all their solicitations. This allows you as a consumer to shop around for the best rate, instead of being misled into accepting a high rate by a slick promotion. The **Fair Credit and Charge Card Disclosure Act of 1988** amends federal law and applies to bank cards, department store cards, and other charge cards, such as American Express and Diner's Club. The law requires that solicitation mailings must "clearly and conspicuously" disclose key financial terms, such as interest rates, fees, grace periods, minimum finance charges, purchase transaction charges, and balance computation methods. You also must get this information when your account is about to be renewed for another year. The only time this law does not apply is when a solicitation is through an ad in a magazine, newspaper, catalog, or "take one" application displayed in a store or restaurant.

This law is designed to let you shop around for the best rate when you get a credit card. You will be surprised how much money you can save by getting a card with a 16% interest rate instead of a 24% interest rate. How do you find out where the best rates are? Read the ads carefully or contact the Bancard Holders of America, 560 Herndon Parkway, Suite 120, Herndon, Virginia 22070 and ask for a list of the lowest cost cards.

# CHAPTER TWO

# Bankruptcy

IT is hard to pick up a newspaper these days without reading that someone or some company has filed bankruptcy. Since the enactment of the new bankruptcy law in 1978, bankruptcy has flourished.

Bankruptcy is one of the most misunderstood areas of law. To many, bankruptcy means failure: "Throw in the towel and try something else!" But, under what is known as Chapter 11 or Chapter 13, bankruptcy can let you stay in business instead of ending it. As with Continental Airlines, bankruptcy may not have any outward effect on the way a company does business. In fact, many businesses are much more successful after their bankruptcy.

Because bankruptcy is so complicated, I can *only begin* to cover this subject. The questions chosen, however, should provide a basic understanding of the types of bankruptcy, and the effect bankruptcy may have on you.

### What is bankruptcy?
### "There are two types."

*Dear Mr. Alderman:*

*I just read that the company that was supposed to remodel my house filed for bankruptcy. Yesterday, they showed up to do the work. I told them I didn't want a bankrupt company working on my house, and they told me we had a contract. The thing I don't understand is how all these companies are still in business if they filed for bankruptcy. I always thought when you filed for bankruptcy you had to sell everything. Am I wrong? Why would a business file bankruptcy and then stay in business?*

You are not entirely wrong, because there are two very different types of bankruptcy. Under the Bankruptcy Code, a business or a person can either file to liquidate their assets, pay their creditors what is owed and start all over, or, they can use the Bankruptcy Code to help them reorganize their financial affairs so that they stay in business and try to pay off their debts. In the first type of bankruptcy, known as a Chapter 7 bankruptcy, a company usually goes out of business. This is what most people think of when they hear the word "bankruptcy." But in the second, known as Chapter 11 for a company and Chapter 13 for an individual, the business continues to operate. Most of the recently publicized bankruptcies have been Chapter 11 bankruptcies, designed to give a company time to pay off its creditors and make a fresh start. For example, Continental and Braniff airlines filed under Chapter 11.

So what happens when someone, or some business, files bankruptcy? First, bankruptcy is controlled by federal law, and all bankruptcies are filed in a special federal court. When a debtor (that is what a business or a person is called when they file bankruptcy) files for a Chapter 7 bankruptcy, he or she agrees to give up all "non-exempt assets" in exchange for a discharge from his or her debts. In Texas this usually means that a person gives up everything except his home and about $60,000 worth of property, in exchange for the release from his debts. (To learn more about exemptions turn to page 51.) The creditors split whatever money there is among them. All the creditors must stop collection efforts, and in most cases the money is divided pro-rata, based on the amount of the debt. *After the Chapter 7 bankruptcy, the debtor usually doesn't owe any money to anyone.* Of course, if you had liens on your property, for example, your house, you would either have to continue to pay or lose the house. And some debts, primarily taxes, are still owed even after bankruptcy.

When a corporation files a Chapter 7 bankruptcy, it usually gives up everything and goes out of business. The creditors split whatever there is and that is the end of it. The corporation no longer exists, and the debts are considered satisfied.

*But under the other type of bankruptcy, a company (or individual) may use the bankruptcy court to get time to reorganize its affairs and try to work things outs.* There are two bankruptcy proceedings that let you do this, a Chapter 11 and a Chapter 13. They are very similar. Under either, once the debtor files, all the creditors have to stop trying to collect and wait for the debtor to propose a payment plan to attempt to pay everyone off. Basically what happens is that the bankruptcy court gives the debtor protection from hungry creditors, while the debtor tries to figure out how to work things out. The main difference between Chapters 11 and 13 is that Chapter 11 is for anyone, corporations and individuals, while Chapter 13 is only available to people with a regular income. A Chapter 13 is sometimes called a wage-earner proceeding. Chapter 13 is the type of bankruptcy you may see in newspaper advertisements with headlines such as "Stop Creditor Harassment . . . File For Protection Under the Federal Bankruptcy Laws."

So to get back to your question: If the company is still in business it must have filed a Chapter 11; or, if it is a sole proprietorship, a Chapter 13. This means that the company has the right to continue in business and, in fact, its contract with you is still enforceable. I suggest that you let them finish the work. If you trusted the company before, there is no less reason to trust them now.

Bankruptcy has taken on a new significance lately. With the assistance of the Bankruptcy Code, debtors can gain valuable time to try to remedy their financial affairs. But bankruptcy laws are very complicated, and some attorneys specialize only in bankruptcy. *If you are considering bankruptcy, make sure you consult with a specialist. Look for an attorney who is "board certified" in consumer bankruptcy.*

### What happens when I file?
### "That depends . . ."

*Dear Mr. Alderman:*
*I really can't believe I'm writing you this letter, but I need your advice. For 20 years I have been a hard-working citizen, and I've never even been late in my payments. I own a house, with a mort-gage, of course, and two cars. My wife and two children have most of the things they need. Now I am suddenly in trouble.*
*About six months ago my employer told me that I had to take a sub-stantial cut in pay or be fired. Any job is better than none, so I agreed to work for less. The following week, we discovered my wife needed surgery. The bills are already over $13,000, and my insur-ance only covers a very small amount. I am behind in all my other bills, and the credit card companies are beginning to hound me.*
*I would like to pay off what I owe, but I don't see how I can do it. Everyone wants to be paid at the same time. I never thought bank-ruptcy was right—a man should pay his bills; but now it seems to be all that is left. What would happen if I filed for bankruptcy?*

First, as I pointed out in the letter right before this one, you should know there are two different types of bankruptcy. In your case, an indi-vidual with a steady income, the choices are a Chapter 7 or a Chapter 13. I will tell you about each in order.

*If you file a Chapter 7, all your creditors must stop trying to collect, you lose all your non-exempt property, and you start all over again, usually not owing anyone a cent.* The purpose of a Chapter 7 is to free you of debt and let you begin fresh. In exchange for being free of your debt, you have to give up non-exempt assets. In Texas this means you can keep your home and up to $60,000 of personal property. If you have anything else, it goes to your creditors. After you file bankruptcy, your creditors share whatever money there is. *After the bankruptcy is over, your creditors cannot try to collect anything from you.* The only significant exception to this would be the bank or finance company that loaned you money to buy your house and car. Because they have a lien on your property, you either have to give it up to pay off the lien, or agree to continue paying after the bankruptcy. One other exception is money owed for taxes or alimony. These debts must still be paid even after bankruptcy.

*A Chapter 7 bankruptcy is a serious matter and you should discuss your particular case with an attorney.* If you feel that you are so hopelessly in debt that the only way to get going again is to clear up all your bills, Chapter 7 may be the thing for you.

But if what you think you need is just more time to work things out with your creditors, you should consider a Chapter 13. In simple terms a Chapter 13 is a court-supervised repayment plan, where all your creditors must leave you alone and let you pay them off over a longer period of time, usually three years. *The first benefit you get from filing a Chapter 13 is that all your creditors must immediately stop trying to collect.* All harassing calls, letters, even lawsuits must stop, and everything goes to the bankruptcy court to be worked out. After you file a Chapter 13, the next step is to come up with a plan to pay everyone back. Usually what you try to do is pay all your creditors less than you are paying now, but over a longer period of time. *You should consider a Chapter 13 only if you think that with some additional time you will be able to get enough money to pay everyone off.* If you know that even with an extra three years you are still too much in debt to pay everyone what you owe them, use a Chapter 7, not a Chapter 13.

*To file bankruptcy you will need the assistance of an attorney.* Talk with him or her before you file, and make sure all your options are considered.

One more thought: There are organizations that help consumers restructure their debt without the need for bankruptcy. These groups are usually called *consumer credit counseling services,* and one of them might be able to give you the assistance you need.

Here is a list of consumer credit counseling agencies throughout the state of Texas. There is usually no charge for their help.

Consumer Credit Counseling Service of Southeast Texas, 4600 Gulf Fwy., Houston, TX 77023, 1-800-873-2227, (713) 923-2227.

Child and Family Services, CCCS Division, 2001 Chicon St., Austin, TX 78722, (512) 478-1648.

Consumer Credit Counseling Center of South Texas, 5842 S. Staples, Corpus Christi, TX 78413, (512) 993-7070.

CCCS of Greater Dallas, Inc., 8737 King George #200, Dallas, TX 75235, (214) 638-2227.

CCCS of Fort Worth, 6100 Western Place #550, Fort Worth, TX 76107, (817) 732-2227.

CCCS of North Central Texas, Inc., 1600 Redbud Blvd. #300, P.O. Box 299, McKinney, TX 75069, 1-800-856-0257.

CCCS of Greater San Antonio, Inc., 4203 Woodcock, Suite 251, San Antonio, TX 78228-1312, (210) 921-2227.

## What happens when someone else files?
### "You may be out of luck!"

*Dear Mr. Alderman:*

*I bought a house for over $70,000 from a local builder. The house was never finished properly and I had problems from the day I moved in. I was finally forced to hire a lawyer, who sued under the Texas Deceptive Trade Practices Act. We won! The court awarded me $36,000, but the builder never paid and now he has filed bankruptcy and gone out of business. What happens next? Am I ever going to get my money? I have since heard that he is back in business, using a different name. Can he do this?*

Unfortunately, I don't have any good news for you. If the builder has filed a Chapter 7 bankruptcy he will be discharged from all his debts, including the money he owes you, and all you get is a pro rata share of his exempt assets. What all this legal jargon means is that the builder doesn't owe you anything and you get to share whatever extra money he had when he filed bankruptcy.

To make sure that you do get whatever is coming, you should file a *proof of claim* with the bankruptcy court. Because you are one of the builder's creditors (anyone he owes money to), you should receive notice from the court of how and where to file your claim. Once you file this simple notice with the bankruptcy court, you will be included in any settlements and get whatever money you are entitled to. But don't expect to receive very much. On the average, creditors in bankruptcy receive only a few cents on the dollar. I should point out that if you are not listed with the court, an unlikely event because of the amount of money you are owed, you are not affected by the bankruptcy.

After the builder has filed bankruptcy he has the right to go back into whatever business he wants, under whatever name he wants. The purpose of bankruptcy is to clear up one's debts and get a fresh start. The builder is now free of his debts and can begin all over. This may not be the way you would want the system to work, and it is often unfair to people like you, but bankruptcy is becoming a more and more popular alternative for people who find they just have to get out from under their debts, and see no other way to do it.

From your letter it appears that the builder filed a Chapter 7 bankruptcy—the type designed to liquidate his assets. However, if the builder filed a Chapter 11, you stand a good chance of being paid, but you should have your attorney help you collect.

## Will bankruptcy clear up my student loans?
### "Probably not."

*Dear Mr. Alderman:*
*I recently graduated from college. I owe over $25,000 in student loans, in addition to my other bills. I am having trouble making ends meet and I am considering filing bankruptcy. How will this affect my student loans?*

Until recently, student loans were not "discharged" in bankruptcy. This meant that even after you filed bankruptcy you would still owe the money for your student loans. The law, however, has now been changed.

The Bankruptcy Code now states that student loans are not discharged, *unless—*

> the loan first became due before five years before the filing of the bankruptcy; or requiring payment will impose an undue hardship on the debtor.

In other words, under the law, your debt probably will not be affected by the bankruptcy if it is less than 5 years old. For example, if you have a student loan that just became due, you probably shouldn't file bankruptcy because you will still owe the loan after the bankruptcy. But if the debt is more than 5 years old, or it is unusually large in comparison to your income, the bankruptcy will wipe it out just as it does most other debts.

## Can a farmer file bankruptcy?
## "Yes. There is a special law."

*Dear Mr. Alderman:*
*I am a small farmer who, like most others, is having problems making ends meet. The other day I heard there was some special bankruptcy law for farmers. Is this true? If it is, can you tell me about it?*

Because of the special hardships faced by farmers, Congress enacted a bankruptcy provision just for them. The law, called Chapter 12, can help stave off farm liquidations and give the farmer more flexibility than ever before.

Chapter 12 is a special section of the Bankruptcy Act just for "family farmers." These are individuals with debts of less than $1.5 million; and 80% of that debt and 50% of income must come from farming. Corporate and partnership farmers also qualify if they are owned by one family.

If you qualify as a family farmer under this law, you can file a petition that operates to immediately stop all of your creditors from taking any action. This is similar to what happens in a Chapter 11; however, Chapter 12 gives you more leeway to determine how your debts will be handled.

The bottom line is that Chapter 12 gives farmers the flexibility needed to rearrange their debts and at the same time continue in business. If you are having serious financial problems, I suggest you speak with an attorney about filing a Chapter 12.

# CHAPTER THREE

# Banks & Banking

FOR most people, checks are considered the same as cash. When you go into a store and the clerk asks, "Cash or charge?" you say cash if you are using a check.

Today nearly everyone who spends money has a checking account. And most of us know the benefits of using a check instead of cash: You have a record of your transactions; and, if the check is lost or stolen, you will not bear the loss the way you would if it had been cash.

Banks handle billions of checks each year and transfer untold amounts of money between accounts. For most of us these transfers go smoothly and we have little need to know, or use, our legal rights against a bank. But we do have substantial legal rights and when something goes wrong you may find that it is the bank, and not you, who has to pay.

### A thief has been using my checks. Do I have to pay?
### "Not unless it was your fault."

*Dear Mr. Alderman:*

*About two weeks ago my purse was stolen in the parking lot of the supermarket. I immediately reported it to the police and then went home and made a list of everything in my wallet. I remembered how important you said it was to notify everyone as soon as possible, so I contacted all my credit card companies. I also called the bank and they told me to come in and close the account and open a new one. The next day I did that and they told me that the thief had written three checks to himself, signed my name, and cashed them that morning. The bank told me that I was responsible for these checks because the forgery was so good there was no way for them to know. This doesn't seem right. Before I go and ask to see the president of the bank, I would like to know what you think. What are my legal rights?*

Under the law, a bank generally has no right to pay checks on which your signature was forged, and if it does it must recredit your account or be responsible for damages. A bank may only pay a check that is "properly payable," and checks with a forged signature are not properly payable. In simple terms, properly payable means in accordance with your instructions; and you did not tell the bank to pay that check—the thief did.

There are a few exceptions to this rule but none of them seem to apply in your case. For example, if your negligence was what made the thief's forgery possible—let's say you carelessly left a signature stamp in a public place—then the bank may not have to pay. Also, if you wait too long to report the forgery, and because of that the bank suffers a loss, you can't complain to the bank.

*Basically, the law is straightforward: A bank may not take your money to pay a check on which your signature is forged. Your account must be recredited and it is up to the bank either to bear the loss or find the thief and try to collect. If your bankers still refuse to give you your money back, take them to small claims court or see a lawyer.*

P.S. If your check is stolen, quickly report the loss to the bank. But there is no need to pay the bank for a stop payment order. As I just explained, it is their loss if they pay.

### My check was signed by someone other than the person I gave it to. Do I still have to pay?
### "Probably not . . . you are entitled to the signature you asked for."

*Dear Mr. Alderman:*
*I owed my next door neighbor $150 for a fence we put up. I gave him a check that he put in his desk. When he went to cash it he realized that it had been stolen. My neighbor has now asked me to give him another check and I am worried about what will happen if the thief cashes or deposits my old check. What are my legal rights if the thief forges my friend's name and my bank pays the check?*

Under the law, a bank that pays a check with a forged endorsement has no right to take your money to cover the check. If they do, you have the right to require them to recredit your account.

For example, suppose your check was made out to "Bob Neighbor." The thief turns over the check and endorses it "Bob Neighbor pay to Tom Thief." Thief then takes the check to his bank and deposits it by signing "Tom Thief." His bank gives him credit for the check and sends it to your bank. Because your bank has no way of knowing that the signatures are not genuine, it will probably pay the check and debit your account. When you get your statement you discover that the check has a forged signature. In the meantime, Thief has taken his money and is gone.

According to the law, once you show the bank that the endorsement is forged, it must recredit your account. The bank then has the right to get the money back from the other bank, and that bank must try to recover from the thief.

What you should do now is contact your bank and ask if the check has been paid. If the check has been paid, explain what happened and ask that they recredit your account. They probably will want you to prove that your neighbor didn't endorse the check and may ask for him to sign an affidavit to that effect. Once they are certain that the signature is a forgery, they will probably recredit your account. If they do not, you have the legal right to compel them to do so.

If the check has not been paid, the bank will probably ask you to put in a stop-payment order. This will ensure that the check is not paid.

As for your neighbor, once you get your money back from the bank, give him another check. Your obligation to pay him still exists.

As I said in the answer right before this one, a bank may take the money in your account only to pay checks that are "properly payable." Checks with forged endorsements are not properly payable, and the bank has no legal right to take your money to pay them.

### How do I stop payment on a check?
### "In Texas, it must be in writing."

*Dear Mr. Alderman:*
*Hello again. I am the same person who wrote you before about the check I gave my next door neighbor that was lost or stolen. I called the bank and they said I had to stop payment. I told them to go ahead and they told me I would have to come down to the bank to do it in writing. They also told me I would have to pay a fee if payment was stopped. Is this the law or is my bank just making things difficult? You know how inconvenient it is to go to a bank during the middle of the day.*

In most states a customer can stop payment over the telephone. Under Texas law, though, an oral stop-payment notice is not binding on the bank. This means that the bank may let you stop payment over the phone, but it is not obligated to do so. As a practical matter most banks will only honor a written stop-payment order.

As to whether your bank may charge you for doing this, the answer is probably yes. Although at least one state attorney general (Michigan) has stated that stop-payment orders are part of the obligation owed a customer and that an additional fee may not be charged, there has been no similar ruling in Texas. *I suggest that you consider the cost of stop-payment orders when you shop for a bank. The cost can vary greatly between banks.*

### The store charged me $25 for a check that bounced. Is this legal? "Probably."

*Dear Mr. Alderman:*

*The other day I bought a CD at my local record shop. It cost $15.95. I paid for it with a check. Unfortunately, I don't balance my checkbook as well as I should and the check bounced. The store called me and told me I owed them $15.95 for the check and $25 for the fact that it bounced. When I went to pay they showed me a sign over the cash register that said: "All returned checks will be charged $25.00!" Is this legal? $25 is a lot of money.*

Based on what you say, the store probably acted lawfully. Under the law a store may charge you up to $25 for a returned check. The store properly posted notice that it would charge a fee for returned checks. As long as the amount is $25 or less, the store acted lawfully.

### My bank just charged me $20 for a bounced check. Is this legal? "There is no specific law governing service charges."

*Dear Mr. Alderman:*

*I know that it isn't right to bounce checks but not everyone is an accountant and sometimes I don't balance my checkbook the way I should. The other day my bank sent me a notice that I bounced a $19 check at a local store. I went right down to the bank and deposited my paycheck and the check that bounced was paid. Now the bank has charged me $20 for bouncing a $19 check. This is crazy. Do they have the right to do this?*

There is no specific law governing what a bank may charge for the services it performs. The cost of the services a bank performs, such as checking accounts, stop-payment orders, and NSF (non-sufficient funds) checks, is governed by basic principles of contract law and the Deceptive Trade Practices Act. *The $20 fee is valid if you voluntarily agreed to pay it—unless the bank deceived or misled you, or the price is unconscionable.* A fee would be unconscionable if it were grossly in excess of the value you received.

For many banks, fees paid for bounced checks represent a substantial source of income, and different banks charge vastly differing amounts—fees as low as $10 or as high as $30 are not unusual. Lawsuits have been filed in other states challenging a bank's right to charge a high fee, but to the best of my knowledge there are no such suits in Texas.

*The best advice I can give you is practical, not legal. Shop around for the bank that has the fairest fees for the services it performs, and, in the future, try to balance your checkbook.*

# CHAPTER FOUR

# Contracts

IN a certain sense, there is *no* such thing as a "contract." You can't buy one, you can't hold it, and you can't pick one up and tote it around. A contract is simply a *legal term* for a promise that the law will enforce. Sometimes this promise will be evidenced by a piece of paper, but that paper is not a contract; the legally enforceable *agreement* is.

Any agreement you enter into may be legally enforceable and may become a contract, no matter what words you may use, and regardless of whether it is oral or written. For example, suppose the neighborhood boy comes by your house and yells: "Hey, lady, want your lawn cut?" A nod of the head will result in a "contract," and after he finishes the task, you will have to pay.

So you see, your life consists of one contract followed by another. When you buy gas for your car, groceries at the store, or have your laundry cleaned, you enter into a contract. Some basic knowledge of contract law should help you with your everyday problems.

As you will find in the next letters, you don't need very specific language, and you usually don't need anything written to enter into a binding contract.

### Must a contract be formal?
### "Just an agreement."

*Dear Mr. Alderman:*
*I own a house at the lake that's about 20 years old. The fence was in need of repairs and my neighbor told me that he would split the costs if I would have the fence repaired. We talked about it for awhile and, ultimately, I agreed to go ahead and have it fixed, and he agreed to pay half. The bill amounted to $350 and now my neighbor refuses to pay. The price, I feel, is very reasonable, but my neighbor says we didn't have any kind of a formal arrangement, and there is nothing I can do. Is he right?*

The law of contracts is not as complicated as many people think. If you agree to do something, in exchange for someone's promise to do something else, there probably is a legally enforceable agreement. To put it simply, if you have intended to be legally bound, you probably are.

In your case, each party made a promise to the other. You promised to fix the fence and he promised to pay you one-half the cost. Based on your letter, it seems that at the time of the agreement you both thought you had entered into a contract. Your agreement is probably legally enforceable.

Contract law long ago dispensed with the need for any formalities before an agreement could be enforceable in a court of law. The modern trend is to enforce every agreement that the parties intended to be binding. You can't get out of a contract by simply saying "I know what I said before, but it wasn't really a formal contract." If your neighbor doesn't pay you the money he owes, I suggest you take him to small claims court. Maybe the judge can convince him that he has entered into a legally enforceable agreement.

### What if she doesn't give me the gift?
### "Not much you can do about it."

*Dear Mr. Alderman:*
*For the past five years my grandmother has been ill. Weekly, I would go to her home and help her with her chores and buy her groceries. Last month she told me that she really appreciated everything that I had done for her, and she wanted me to have her diamond pin. Yesterday, I went to her house and asked about the pin. She said she had changed her mind and given it to my sister. My dear sibling has never done anything for my grandmother. Is there any way I can make my grandmother keep her promise?*
*P.S. I even have a written promise that reads: "In exchange for the love and affection shown to me by my granddaughter, Betsy, I promise to give her my diamond pin, before the end of the year."*

The fact that you have a signed, written promise does not mean that you can force the person to do what he promised to do. *As a general rule, promises to make a gift are not enforceable.* This is because of the legal doctrine known as "consideration."

Under the law, a promise is enforceable only if it is given in exchange for something. In legalese there must be a "quid pro quo"—something for something. For example, suppose that I promise to pay you to paint my house. What we have actually done is exchange promises. I have promised to pay you in return for your promise to paint. We have each given something in exchange for something else. The promises are enforceable and we have a contract. The exchange, however, must be for something in the future. If you promise to pay someone for something that has already happened, the promise is not enforceable—it is a promise to make a gift. For example, if you paint my house without my asking, and after you finish I say, "You did a good job, I promise to pay you next week," the promise would not be enforceable because it was not made in exchange for performance. For every enforceable promise there is a "quid pro quo," something exchanged for something else.

So what does all this mean to you? Your grandmother was promising to make you a gift for what you had done in the past—and such promises cannot be enforced in a court of law. Even though your grandmother may be morally bound to give you the pin, there is no legally enforceable obligation. Things would be different, though, if your grandmother had said, "If you help me with the groceries, I will give you my pin." In that case there would be a legally enforceable promise because she was making her promise in exchange for yours.

*The bottom line is that not all promises, even those in writing, are enforceable. If someone promises to give you a gift and doesn't, you usually can't force him to pay.*

There is, however, one exception to this that you should know. If you rely on the promise, and suffer a loss, you may be able to force the person to compensate you for your loss. For example, suppose your grandmother told you she was going to give you $500 to buy a coat, and relying on this you put down a $50 nonrefundable deposit. If your grandmother changed her mind you couldn't force her to pay the $500, but you could collect the $50 you spent in reliance on her promise.

### Is a contract valid if I don't sign?
### "It probably doesn't matter."

*Dear Mr. Alderman:*
*My driveway was in need of repair, so I called a contractor to fix it. We discussed what he would do, and he sent me an estimate of $1,500. I phoned him back and told him to go ahead and begin work. The next day, when he arrived with his crew, I informed him that I had changed my mind and that I was going to fix it myself. He was*

*very mad and told me that he was going to lose $100 because he had to pay his crew for showing up. I told him I was sorry, that it wasn't my fault and, besides, we never had a real contract because I never signed anything. I have now received a letter informing me that he is planning to sue me in small claims court for the $100. Since I didn't sign anything, do I have to pay?*

Most people are surprised to find out that they usually don't have to sign anything to have an enforceable contract. In your case, your contract was for the performance of a service and such contracts do not require a signature *unless they can't be performed within a year.* Your contract clearly was to be performed in less than a year, and you are responsible for any loss the contractor incurred.

Under the law, most contracts do not have to be in writing, or be signed, to be enforceable. But some contracts are considered more important than others, and there is a law called the Statute of Frauds that requires that certain kinds of contracts be "evidenced" by a signed writing. The most common types of contracts that need a signed writing are: contracts for the sale of land; contracts that cannot be performed within one year; contracts for the sale of goods that cost over $500; and contracts to pay the debts of another. To enforce these types of contracts it is necessary that there be some writing sufficient to show that a contract has been made and signed by the person against whom the contract is being enforced. A brief example will show you how this law works.

Suppose that I agree to sell you my house. Because contracts for the sale of land are covered by the Statute of Frauds, the agreement is not enforceable unless we have a writing. We orally agree to the sale, and I then go home and write you a letter telling you how excited I am about the deal, and discussing all the details. I sign the letter and mail it to you. At this point there is an enforceable contract against me, because I signed a writing, indicating that we made a contract, and giving the important terms. But the contract probably would not be enforceable against you because you did not sign anything. *If you are worried about the enforceability of an agreement, protect yourself: Put it in writing.*

The Statute of Frauds is designed to prevent one person from forcing another into contract by falsely stating that they had an agreement. Without the writing the agreement is not enforceable. But the law does not like people to use the Statute of Frauds to get out of contracts that they made and that the other person relied on. For example, suppose you agreed to buy a custom-made boat from me at a cost of $2,500. After I build the boat, you change your mind and say you won't pay. The contract is for the sale of goods that cost over $500, so I need a signed writing to sue you. Am I out of luck? Not in this case. There are many exceptions to the law that requires a writing, and this is one of them. Because the goods were specially manufactured, I can sue you even without the writing. All I have to do is prove you orally agreed. The same rule applies whenever one party has performed his part of the deal and then the other party tries to get out of the contract.

*Remember, most contracts do not require a writing. Even when a writing is required, the requirement may be waived if it is unfair to one of the parties. Best advice: If you make an oral contract, be prepared to keep your promise.*

### Does an agreement to split lottery winnings have to be in writing? "Probably not."

*Dear Mr. Alderman:*
*Several of my friends and I buy lottery tickets each week. Each of us puts in two dollars, and we buy ten tickets. We have agreed that if we win we will split the winnings between us. I know it is unlikely, but if we did win, could I force everyone to split the money? Do we have to have a written agreement?*

You have the right to force everyone to divide the money, provided you can convince a court that you really did make the agreement. Basically, you and your friends have entered into a contract. The terms of the contract are that each of you will provide part of the proceeds to buy the tickets and, if you win, you will divide the proceeds equally.

This agreement is enforceable without any form of a writing. As I stated in the prior letter, most contracts do not have to be in writing to be enforceable. This contract, because it could be performed in less than one year, is an example of one type of contract that does not have to be in writing. You would need a writing, however, if your agreement to buy tickets was for more than one year and did not end even if you won the lottery earlier.

This does not mean, however, that it would not be a good idea to put your agreement in a written form. Even though your agreement is enforceable, there still may be problems proving it if you were to win. The best way to avoid any problems in the future is to write an agreement and have everyone sign it.

## What if he doesn't do what he promised?
## "No punishment."

*Dear Mr. Alderman:*

*I signed a contract to purchase a stereo from a local store. When I went back the following day to pick it up, the manager told me he had just sold the stereo to another customer and that he couldn't get another one for several weeks. I was really mad . . . since I knew the manager didn't like me and had sold it just for spite. I went to another store, right around the corner, and I bought the same stereo for a much better price. Now I want to know if there is anything I can do about the fact that the store manager didn't sell me the original stereo. I have a written contract.*

The law of contracts is designed to do one thing: ensure that you get the benefit of your bargain. If someone breaches a contract, you are entitled to money damages to put you in the same place you would have been in if the contract were performed. *It is very rare that punitive damages are awarded for breach of contract. All the law requires is that the breaching party put the other party in as good a position as he would be in if the contract had been performed.*

In your case, you are better off after the store breached the contract than you would have been had the store performed, so you are not entitled to any damages. If you had to pay more for the stereo at the other store, you could recover the difference in price. But in your case, you saved money. Even though you have a written contract, you cannot get any kind of a penalty from the merchant for not living up to his part of the bargain.

The damages for breach of contract can be demonstrated in this way:

| | |
|---|---|
| market price | (what it will cost you to get the same thing somewhere else) |
| − contract price | (what you would have paid) |
| = damages | |
| + consequential loss | (whatever else you lost because of the breach) |
| = total recovery | |

For example, suppose the stereo cost $100 more at every other store and you had to drive an extra 50 miles to find one. You would then be entitled to $100 (the difference between the market price and the contract price) plus a reasonable amount for your mileage (a consequential loss).

In your case, though, the formula results in a negative number, and even though you don't owe the store, it doesn't have to pay you any damages.

*The law requires that you perform any contract you enter into, but damages are designed to compensate, not punish. If the other party's breach didn't hurt you economically, you are probably not entitled to any damages.*

## I couldn't afford to pay for my layaway.
## Don't I get my money back?
## "It depends."

*Dear Mr. Alderman:*
*A few months ago I saw a great dress at a little store near my house. I asked if they did layaways, and they said yes. They gave me something to sign, told me I had to pay $5 a week and that in 12 weeks the dress would be mine. The dress was marked $60, so this seemed fair. I paid for seven weeks and then lost my job. When I went back and told them I couldn't make the payments anymore, they said, "Fine, we keep your money and the dress." Then they showed me the paper I signed that said they could do this. I know I should have read it before I signed, but I just assumed that if I stopped paying, I would get my money back. Is there anything I can do?*

You asked a good question, and I was surprised that I couldn't find a Texas law dealing directly with the area of layaways. It is a matter of private contract between you and the store. Whatever you agree to is enforceable as any other contract would be. *It is very important that you carefully read the agreement before you sign it.*

Nevertheless, this does not mean that the store has the right to do whatever it wants. They are still subject to the Texas Deceptive Trade Practices Act. Under this law, they would be liable if they misrepresented the terms of the agreement. For example, if they told you that you would get your money back, they could not hold you to a written agreement that said otherwise. In that case, by keeping your money, they would violate the Deceptive Trade Practices Act, and you could get three times your damages. (Read Chapter Ten.) This law also prohibits them from doing anything "unconscionable." This is defined as any act that results in a "gross disparity between the value received and the consideration paid." In your case, you have paid $35 and all you have received is the right to pay off the dress over time, instead of all at once. I would agree that this has some value, but not that much. Based upon the practices of other stores, you may be able to show that this right is worth no more than 10% of the purchase price. In my opinion, a layaway plan that lets the store keep all of the money and the goods when you don't pay the full amount is unconscionable. Charging a small fee for the right to use a layaway would be a much fairer approach.

If you think you were deceived, or that the amount you were charged is unconscionable under the Deceptive Trade Practices Act, you should consider letting the store know and going to small claims court, if necessary. Remember, though, before you use this law, there are certain things you must do, so read pages 104 to 106 carefully.

### Who owns my dental records?
### "Your dentist."

*Dear Mr. Alderman:*

*I recently changed dentists. In order to avoid having additional X-rays, I asked my former dentist for the X-rays he had. He refused to give them to me. Can he do this? I paid for the X-rays; aren't they mine?*

Under the law, what you paid for were the services of the dentist. The records of the dentist, including X-rays, belong to the dentist. If he or she does not want to give them to you, you have no right to them.

I understand your desire not to have additional X-rays, and many dentists will allow their patients to take their X-rays to another dentist. I suggest you speak with your dentist once more and explain why you want the X-rays. Perhaps you can work something out.

### Should I co-sign a note for my friend?
### "Being a co-signer can be dangerous."

*Dear Mr. Alderman:*

*A very good friend of mine is having a problem getting credit because of financial problems she had over two years ago. She is now back on her feet but still has a bad credit report. She has asked me to co-sign a note to buy a car. I fully trust this person and know that she will pay.*

*Recently, however, someone told me that if my friend doesn't pay it could hurt my credit. Is this true? Can her default show up on my credit report?*

Being a co-signer may seem like the "nice" thing to do, but unfortunately the old saying "no good deed goes unpunished," often applies to co-signers. When you co-sign or guarantee someone else's signature, you are in effect agreeing to the same obligation they are. If they do not pay, you must. And if you do not, it will be reflected on your credit report. In other words, don't co-sign unless you are willing to bear full responsibility for the obligation.

I should point out, however, that you are not without any recourse if you must pay. If you, as a co-signer, pay, you are entitled to seek recovery against the person who was primarily responsible on the note. For example, if your friend didn't pay and you had to, you would be entitled to reimbursement from your friend.

### How long do I have to change my mind after I sign a contract? "Usually no time!"

*Dear Mr. Alderman:*

*Last week I went to buy a new car. It was late at night, and after a very hard sell, I signed a contract. The next morning I thought about the terms and decided they were more than I really could afford. When I called the car dealer to cancel, he said I couldn't. I thought you had three days to get out of a contract after you signed it. Isn't that the law in Texas?*

No. In fact, as far as I know, it isn't the law anywhere. In most cases, once you sign a contract you are obligated by its terms. Unless you were tricked, deceived, or defrauded into signing the agreement, you are usually bound. (Read the material in Chapter Ten if this is the case.)

*The existence of a three-day "cooling-off" period is one of the most widely held misconceptions about the law.* There are only very limited instances in which you have three days to change your mind. For example, you have this right if you sign a contract that puts a lien on your home, a contract for time-share property, a health spa contract, or most contracts that are negotiated door-to-door. In other cases, though, once you sign you are bound.

The bottom line is simple. Don't sign anything until you have had time to read it and think about it. And as far as that high-pressure salesperson is concerned, go home and really think about the deal. If it really is a good deal, it will still be there the next day.

### How can I get out of a long-term health club contract?
### "There is a law."

*Dear Mr. Alderman:*

*Like everyone else, my New Year's resolution was to get back in shape. The first thing I did was rush off to the local health club to sign up. The salesperson told me that they had a "special" that day and it would only be $19.99 a month. He told me that to save time I should just sign the forms and he would have them ready for me when I came back that afternoon. I signed and then picked them up a few hours later. When I got home, I was shocked to see that it was $19.99 a month, plus an initiation fee of $300. I don't have that kind of money. When I called and told him I wanted to cancel, his manager told me a contract is a contract and I should have read it before I signed. What can I do? Is this just an expensive lesson to not sign anything before you read it?*

Although learning not to sign blank forms is a good lesson to learn, it is not all you can do in this case. Texas has a Health Spa Act that protects you. Basically, this law protects against false and deceptive acts or misrepresentations, such as what you describe. More importantly, this law has a cooling-off period and requires that health clubs post a bond with the secretary of state.

Under the law, any health spa contract must give you three days to cancel. The law requires that notice of this be in bold print in the contract. The law also requires a bold notice telling consumers not to sign a contract with any blanks.

I suggest you contact the manager again and let her know you know about this law. If she doesn't agree to cancel it, you should file a complaint with the secretary of state. That is the office that enforces this law and keeps the bond health clubs must file.

# CHAPTER FIVE

# Credit Cards

IN Chapter One, you saw how important credit is, and that there are laws to help you obtain credit at a fair price. But once you have the credit, all sorts of complications can arise while using it.

Have you ever wondered if you could stop payment on a credit card the same way you can on a check? Or who is responsible when your credit card is stolen and the tacky thief enjoys an around-the-world cruise—via *your* charge cards?

As you will see, credit cards offer more protection than any other payment plan.

### Do I have to pay if the plant has mites?
### "Luckily, you used a credit card."

*Dear Mr. Alderman:*

*Approximately three weeks ago, I bought a new houseplant. It was quite expensive, and the local florist told me it was in excellent shape and, with good care, would be a real "showpiece." Shortly after I got it home, I noticed it had a horrible case of spider mites. The plant was so infested I couldn't even bring it into the house. The next day, I returned it to the florist, who told me the mites must have come from my house "as his plants were all spotless." I told him the plant was never in my house and it was obvious that the mites had been there for a long period of time. He said he was sorry, but he wasn't going to do anything and, according to him, I could have the plant back or leave it with him. He then laughed and said: "Remember the old maxim 'caveat emptor' let the buyer beware." At any rate, last week I received my credit card bill with the $80 charge for the plant on it. Is there anything I can do?*

If you had paid for the plant with cash, your only remedy would be to try to get the merchant to refund your money, or go to small claims court. But luckily you used a credit card, and as you will see, this gives you substantial rights. Under federal law, a charge card company is not allowed to recover any amount from you that the merchant would not be allowed to recover. In legal jargon, the card company takes the account subject to all "claims and defenses" the buyer has against the merchant.

What this means is that you have a chance to explain to the charge card company why you don't want to pay. For example: If the florist were to try to collect the $80 from you, you would be able to refuse, saying the goods were defective and did not live up to the promise of being show quality.

Under the law, the charge card company is treated like the merchant. You can say to the charge card company: "I don't have to pay my bill, because the goods I purchased, and tried to return, are defective." You have this right against the charge card company *until you pay the charge* and if the following three conditions have been met:

1. You have made a good faith effort to settle the matter with the merchant.
2. The goods cost over $50.
3. The sale took place within your home state or within 100 miles of your home address.

This law protects you whenever you pay for goods or services with a charge card. If you receive your bill and there is a charge for goods or services that you did not receive or that were defective, you should immediately contact the charge card company, in writing, and tell them of the dispute.

*Do not pay the charge you are disputing!*

You must write the credit card company and explain that you are disputing the charge. Check the back of your billing statement for the proper address. Sometimes the credit card company will listen to your version of the dispute over the phone. But in order to fully retain all your rights under the law, follow up any phone call with a letter sent via certified mail, return receipt requested, confirming the call.

The law we are discussing is called the **Fair Credit Billing Act.** To find out how to use this law, read the next letter.

### What can I do when a company goes bankrupt? "Next time, use a credit card."

*Dear Mr. Alderman:*
*It seems like every day another business is going bankrupt, or just disappearing. I am worried that I am going to buy something from*

*a business and before it is delivered the company will go bankrupt.*
*Some of my friends are stuck with tickets on bankrupt airlines. How*
*can I protect myself?*

As a consumer, there is no way you can prevent a company from going
bankrupt, but by using an alternative payment method, the credit card,
you can usually protect yourself from having to bear any loss. Under the
Fair Credit Billing Act, a credit card company may not collect for goods
or services that you purchased but never received. The same rule would
probably apply if you charged a plane ticket, and you never have an
opportunity to use it because the airline has gone bankrupt, canceling
your flight.

The law is easy to use, but you must follow a few simple rules.

First:
>  You must send a separate, written billing error notice to the card
>  company. (Your billing insert will give you the address.)

Second:
>  Your notice must reach the card company within 60 days after the
>  first bill containing the error was mailed to you.

These steps must be explained in your bill. Usually there will be a
statement like the following:

### BILLING RIGHTS SUMMARY
### (In Case of Errors or Questions About Your Bill)

If you think your bill is wrong, or if you need more information
about a transaction on your bill, write us (on a separate sheet) at (the
address shown on your bill) as soon as possible. We must hear from
you no later than 60 days after we sent you the first bill on which the
error or problem appeared. You can telephone us, but doing so will not
preserve your rights. In your letter, give us the following information:

• Your name and account number.

• The dollar amount of the suspected error.

• A description of the error and explain, if you can, why you
  believe there is an error. If you need more information, describe
  the item you are unsure about.

You do not have to pay any amount in question while we are
investigating, but you are still obligated to pay the parts of your bill
that are not in question. While we investigate your question, we can-

not report you as delinquent or take any action to collect the amount you question.

## Special Rule For Credit Card Purchases

If you have a problem with the quality of goods or services that you purchased with a credit card, and you have tried in good faith to correct the problem with the merchant, you may not have to pay the remaining amount due on the goods or services. You have this protection only when the purchase price was more than $50 and the purchase was made in your home state or within 100 miles of your mailing address. (If we own or operate the merchant, or if we mailed you the advertisement for the property or services, all purchases are covered regardless of amount or location of purchase.)

You may use the following form for your letter. Send this letter to your credit card company at the address listed on your monthly statement. Send it via certified mail, return receipt requested:

---

Date                                                                Your name
                                                                    Address

Credit Card Company
Address
RE: Account #_____

I am disputing the charge in my (<u>month</u>) statement in the amount of $(<u>give amount</u>), for the purchase of (<u>item</u>).

*State reasons for refusal to pay. For example, the writer of
the prior letter would say:*

This charge was for the purchase of a plant which the store told me was in great condition, a showpiece. The plant was infected with mites. I have returned the plant and refuse to pay because it is defective. The store now has the plant.

Please remove this charge from my bill. Thank you for your expected cooperation.

_____
Signed

---

Next time you buy goods or services, think about the advantages of using your credit card. If the goods or services never arrive or the company goes out of business, you will not have to bear a loss because the law allows you to dispute your bill and assert your legal rights against the credit card company.

## THE FAIR CREDIT BILLING ACT

The Fair Credit Billing Act (FCBA) protects you in the case of "billing errors." Billing errors are defined by the law, and include:

1. Charges not made by you or anyone authorized to use your account.
2. Charges which are incorrectly identified or for which the wrong amount or date is shown.
3. Charges for goods or services which you did not accept or which were not delivered as agreed.
4. Computational or similar errors.
5. Failure to properly reflect payments or other credits, such as returns.
6. Not mailing or delivering bills to your current address (provided you give a change of address at least 20 days before the billing period ends).
7. Charges for which you request an explanation or written proof of purchase.

*This law applies to any business you have an account with, including stores, credit card companies, and even bank overdraft checking accounts.* If you feel a billing error has occurred, you must send the creditor a billing error notice. This notice must reach the creditor within 60 days after you receive the first bill containing the error. Send the notice to the address provided on your bill. In your letter you should include the following information:

1. Name and account number.
2. A statement that you believe your bill contains an error and that includes the dollar amount involved.
3. A statement describing why you think there is a mistake.

The law requires only that you *send* this notice, but to protect yourself, send it *certified mail,* return receipt requested.

## What must the creditor do?

The creditor must acknowledge your letter claiming a billing error within 30 days after he has received it unless, of course, the problem is resolved within that time period. In any event, within two billing cycles (but not more than 90 days), the creditor must conduct a reasonable investigation and either correct the mistake or explain why he believes the bill to be correct.

## What happens while a bill is being disputed?

You may withhold payment of the amount in dispute, including the affected portions of minimum payments and finance charges, until the dispute is resolved. You are still required to pay any part of the bill which is not disputed, including finance and other charges.

While the FCBA dispute settlement procedure is going on, the creditor cannot take any legal or other action to collect the disputed amount. Your account cannot be closed or restricted in any way, except that the disputed amount may be applied against your credit limit.

## What about your credit rating?

While a bill is being disputed, the creditor cannot threaten to damage your credit rating or report you as delinquent to anyone. The creditor is, however, permitted to report that you are disputing your bill.

Another federal law, the **Equal Credit Opportunity Act,** prohibits creditors from discriminating against credit applicants who, in good faith, exercise their rights under the FCBA. You cannot be denied credit merely because you have disputed a bill.

## What if the creditor makes a mistake?

If your bill is found to contain a billing error, the creditor must write to you, explaining the corrections to be made on your account. In addition to crediting your account with the amount not owed, the creditor must remove all finance charges, late fees, or other charges relating to the amount. If the creditor concludes that you owe part of the disputed amount, this too must be explained in writing. You also have the right to request copies of documents proving you owe the money.

## What if the bill is correct?

If the creditor investigates and still believes the bill to be correct, you must be told promptly, in writing, how much you owe and why. You may also request copies of relevant documents. At this point, you will owe the disputed amount, plus any finance charges accumulated while the amount was being disputed.

## What if you still disagree?

Even after the Fair Credit Billing Act dispute settlement procedure has ended, you may still feel the bill is wrong. If this happens, write to the creditor within 10 days after receiving the explanation, stating that you refuse to pay the disputed amount. At this point, the creditor may begin collection procedures. If the creditor, however, reports you to a credit bureau as delinquent, he must also state that you do not think you owe the money. You must also be told who receives such reports.

## What if the creditor doesn't follow the procedures?

Any creditor who fails to follow strictly the Fair Credit Billing Act dispute settlement procedure is penalized by not being allowed to collect the first $50 of the amount in dispute, even if the bill turns out to be correct. For example: This penalty would apply if a creditor acknowledges your complaint in 45 days (15 days too late) or takes more than two billing cycles to resolve a dispute. It also applies if a creditor threatens to report, or "improperly" reports, your billing situation. Thus, if you owed $200, the creditor's delay would mean it can only recover $150.00.

*The bottom line is: Use a credit card whenever you have any doubts about a company, or whenever you are buying something to arrive, or to be used, in the future.*

## Don't I have to give my consent for someone to get my credit report?
## "No."

*Dear Mr. Alderman:*
*I recently learned that a mortgage company got a copy of my credit report. I was never told they were doing this. It was my impression that anyone who requested a credit check needed my permission. Am I wrong?*

Yes. Under the Fair Credit Reporting Act, a company can get a copy of your report if they are using the report to furnish you credit or review your account. Credit reports may also be provided in connection with employment and insurance. Based on what you say in your letter, the mortgage company had a legitimate basis for requesting the report and, therefore, was entitled to it.

The best way to find out who has requested a copy of your report is to contact the credit bureau. They keep records of who has made an inquiry. If you feel a report was requested for unlawful reasons, you should let the credit bureau and the Federal Trade Commission know.

### What happens when my card is stolen?
### "Good news for you."

*Dear Mr. Alderman:*

*The other day I went into a restaurant and paid for my meal with a credit card. The waiter had me sign the receipt but forgot to return my card. I didn't discover this until several days later when I went to charge another meal and found the card missing. Of course, I immediately called the restaurant and was told the waiter had been fired. I called the credit card company and told them my card was stolen, and they told me to write a letter confirming this. Now I am worried about what will happen if my card is used by the waiter.*

Don't worry. Federal law protects you when your credit card is lost or stolen. Under the law, your *maximum* liability for the unauthorized use of your credit card is $50. But that liability may be even less if you quickly notify the credit card company. You have no liability for charges incurred after you have given the company notice that your card was stolen or lost. Notice may be given in any reasonable way, *including over the telephone*. In your case, you will not have to pay for any charges after the date you phoned the card company, and the most you will have to pay for unauthorized charges made before you gave notice is $50.

If you want to make certain you never have to pay anything if your credit card is lost or stolen, keep the telephone number for the credit card company handy and call as soon as you find your card is missing. A quick phone call could save you $50.

*Good advice: Make a photostatic copy of the contents of your wallet so you can quickly report any lost or stolen credit cards.*

### Someone is charging things to my account. What are my rights?
### "You may not have to pay anything."

*Dear Mr. Alderman:*

*I recently received my credit card bill and there were three charges for things I didn't buy. I disputed the charges as you suggested and was told they were for mail order items charged to my account and sent to someone else. The store said that it was a phone order and they got my account number that way. I didn't make these calls and I don't feel I should have to pay anything, even the $50.*

I agree; I think you are correct. Under the law you don't have to pay for any *unauthorized* charge. A store that simply accepts a credit card number over the phone, and mails the merchandise to a different address runs the risk that the card holder won't pay. I suggest you make it clear to the credit card company that you did not order the items and that you do not intend to pay.

As far as the $50 is concerned, I don't think you should have to pay even that much. As I stated on page 46, if you *lose* your card or it is *stolen,* you may be required to pay up to the first $50. This rule doesn't apply when someone fraudulently uses your number, but not the card. In other words, the law imposes some obligations on you if you are careless and lose the card, or it is stolen. But as long as you have the card you have no liability for the unauthorized use of your card number.

### I lost my bank card—what now?
### "All plastic is not equal."

*Dear Mr. Alderman:*

*I recently used a walk-up teller machine to get some cash. I withdrew $50 and left. Apparently I dropped my card, because I can't find it. I have looked everywhere, but it is just missing. I remember reading something about the fact that I am only liable for $50 if I lose my credit card. Am I protected if someone finds my bank card and uses it?*

No! The law protecting you in the case of lost credit cards does not apply to cards that electronically transfer money directly out of your account. Unlike a credit card, which extends credit during the period between the time of making the charge and the time you pay the bill, a bank card immediately debits your account.

*Remember: The law regarding bank cards such as MPACT or Pulse is very different from the law regarding credit cards.* If your bank card is lost or stolen, *your liability depends upon how quickly you report the loss.* Your liability is limited to $50, *only if* you notify the institution *within two business* days of learning of the loss. If you wait, your liability may be as high as $500. And, should you fail to report the loss within 60 days after your statement is mailed to you, you are responsible for all transfers made after 60 days (even if it is over $500). This means you could lose all the money in your account, plus any overdraft protection you may have with the bank.

For example, suppose your automated teller machine card is stolen by some nefarious thief who has also discovered your code number. (*Remember: A good way to protect yourself is to keep your code number a secret.*) The first stop the villain makes is at the ATM where he promptly withdraws $75 from your account. The next day, he returns and withdraws a hefty $200 (he's getting greedy!). A week later you attempt to use your card only to discover it's missing.

If you call the bank within two business days after you discover the card missing, all you lose is $50. But, should you wait a week, you will be responsible for the entire $275; if you wait longer you may lose all of the money in your account. For instance, many people put their bank statement aside, planning to find a "free moment" later to look it over. Meanwhile, two-and-a-half months go by. The thief decides to hit the ATM again and, with your card and code in hand, wipes out your entire account, which amounts to $1,000. Because you did not report the discrepancy in your statement within 60 days after the bank mailed the statement, the entire loss will fall on your shoulders.

*Remember: A delay of two days in reporting the loss of a debit card could cost you $500. Promptly review all bank statements and report any unauthorized transfer of funds.*

The law regulating misuse of bank cards is called the **Electronic Fund Transfer Act.** It covers not only your bank cards, but also any pre-authorized payments you allow the bank to make. For example, many of us are using electronic fund transfers to have some of our regular monthly payments made automatically, such as mortgage payments. Electronic fund transfers are expected to replace checks as the most common way to do business in the future. Soon we will be paying for our groceries at the supermarket with a card that automatically deducts the money from our account and transfers it to the supermarket's account.

If you would like more information about electronic funds transfers and your rights, you may send for this free booklet:

"Alice in Debit-Land"
Board of Governors
Federal Reserve System
Washington, DC 20551

# CHAPTER SIX

# Debt Collection

EVERYONE will surely agree that we should all pay our bills, and that they should be paid on time. But once in a while things happen and somehow we just can't. If you are unable to pay all of your bills all of the time, you should know that federal and state laws exist to protect you from unscrupulous debt collectors.

Most consumers pay their debts. Even though less than two percent of all consumer credit obligations ever become delinquent, late or unpaid accounts total several billions of dollars. As one might expect, with this vast sum of money at stake, debt collectors often devote considerable energy to collection of delinquent debts, and some of their efforts are illegal.

Debt collection usually begins with a polite letter from the company informing the late party that the bill is overdue and requesting payment, or at least requesting a payment plan. If nothing can be resolved, additional letters will be sent telling the debtor of more drastic actions to follow.

But if the letters fail to get the needed funds, the account is usually forwarded to a collection agency. The correspondence, at this point, will become more urgent and the tone more harsh. The debtor also may receive telephone calls, both at home and at work, pleading for payment. If payment does not result, the next step is to turn the matter over to an attorney who will file suit. But suing is expensive and only used as a last resort. If possible, the debt collector wants to be paid without going to court, and sometimes this means resorting to more forceful, and often illegal, means.

The ingenuity of debt collectors is unlimited and, unfortunately, their approach is oftentimes questionable. Tales of the misconduct of debt collectors could fill the pages of many books. Finally, aggressive tactics of some of them became so abusive that Congress found it necessary to pass a law to protect debtors. This law is called the **Fair Debt Collection Practices Act,** and it provides protection to consumers who experience harassing and threatening conditions at the hands of pesty debt-collectors. This law, along with the **Texas Debt Collection Act,** should ensure that honest debtors, who are trying to do their best but just get in a little over their heads, are treated fairly and humanely by debt collectors.

Before talking about these laws, however, you should know what legal rights your creditors have if they do sue you. As the first letter shows, Texas law is very generous to debtors.

## What can the debt collector get?
## "Not very much."

*Dear Mr. Alderman:*

*I owe a local department store about $1,000. I have been unable to pay in full and, even though I send them as much as I can each month, they have told me they are going to sue me. I have a steady job and a small house with a large mortgage. Every penny I earn goes to pay my bills. If they do sue, what can they get from me?*

Every state has a law that "exempts" some of a debtor's property from his creditors. Exempt property is property your creditors can never take. No matter how much money you owe, there is some property that the state feels is so important to you that you should be able to keep it. *Texas has about the most favorable exemption statutes in the country.* Under Texas law your creditors cannot take your homestead or a specified amount of personal property, in most cases up to $60,000. Here is what the law says:

PERSONAL PROPERTY EXEMPTION

(a) Personal property, as described in Section 42.002, is exempt from garnishment, attachment, execution, or other seizure if:
   (1) the property is provided for a family and has an aggregate fair market value of not more than $60,000, exclusive of the amount of any liens, security interests, or other charges encumbering the property; or
   (2) the property is owned by a single adult, who is not a member of a family, and has an aggregate fair market value of not more than $30,000, exclusive of the amount of any liens, security interests, or other charges encumbering the property.
(b) The following personal property is exempt from seizure and is not included in the aggregate limitations prescribed by Subsection (a):

(1) current wages for personal services, except for the enforcement of court-ordered child support payments;

(2) professionally prescribed health aids of a debtor or a dependent of a debtor.

(c) This section does not prevent seizure by a secured creditor with a contractual landlord lien or other security in the property to be seized.

(d) Unpaid commissions for personal services not to exceed 25 percent of the aggregate limitations prescribed by Subsection (a) are exempt from seizure and are included in the aggregate.

## Personal Property

(a) The following personal property is exempt under Section 42.001(a):

(1) home furnishings, including family heirlooms;

(2) provisions for consumption;

(3) farming or ranching vehicles and implements;

(4) tools, equipment, books, and apparatus, including boats and motor vehicles used in a trade or profession;

(5) wearing apparel;

(6) jewelry not to exceed 25 percent of the aggregate limitations prescribed by Section 12.001(a);

(7) two firearms;

(8) athletic and sporting equipment, including bicycles;

(9) a two-wheeled or four-wheeled motor vehicle for each member of family or single adult who holds a driver's license or who does not hold a driver's license but who relies on another person to operate the vehicle for the benefit of the nonlicensed person;

(10) the following animals and forage on hand for their consumption:

(A) two horses, mules, or donkeys and a saddle, blanket, and bridle for each;

(B) 12 head of cattle;

(C) 60 head of other types of livestock; and

(D) 120 fowl;

(11) household pets; and

(12) the present value of any life insurance policy to the extent that a member of the family of the insured or a dependent of

a single insured adult claiming the exemption is beneficiary of the policy.

(b) Personal property, unless precluded from being encumbered by other law, may be encumbered by a security interest under Section 9.203, Business & Commerce Code, or Sections 41 and 42, Certificate of Title Act (Article 6687-1, Vernon's Texas Civil Statutes), or by a lien fixed by other law, and the security interest or lien may not be avoided on the ground that the property is exempt under this chapter.

## INTERESTS IN LAND EXEMPT FROM SEIZURE

(a) A homestead and one or more lots used for a place of burial of the dead are exempt from seizure for the claims of creditors except for encumbrances properly fixed on homestead property.

(b) Encumbrances may be properly fixed on homestead property for:
   (1) purchase money;
   (2) taxes on the property; or
   (3) work and material used in constructing improvements on the property if contracted for in writing as provided by Sections 53.059(a), (b), and (c).

(c) The homestead claimant's proceeds of a sale of a homestead are not subject to seizure for a creditor's claim for six months after the date of sale.

## Definition of Homestead

(a) If used for the purposes of an urban home or as a place to exercise a calling or business in the same urban area, the homestead of a family or a single, adult person, not otherwise entitled to a homestead, shall consist of not more than one acre of land which may be in one or more lots, together with any improvements thereon.

(b) If used for the purposes of a rural home, the homestead shall consist of:
   (1) for a family, not more than 200 acres, which may be in one or more parcels, with the improvements thereon; or
   (2) for a single, adult person, not otherwise entitled to a homestead, not more than 100 acres, which may be in one or more parcels, with the improvements thereon.

(c) A homestead is considered to be rural if, at the time the designation is made, the property is not served by municipal utilities and fire and police protection.

(d) The definition of a homestead as provided in this section applies to all homesteads in this state whenever created.

*So what does all this mean to you?* In summary, it means that you can keep your home, free from all your creditors except the one that loaned you the money to buy the house and any that are owed money for improving it. If you don't pay these debts, or if you don't pay your taxes, you may be forced to sell your house to pay your debts. You also can keep personal property, up to $60,000 for a family, so long as the property is included in the list and you didn't voluntarily give your creditor a lien. For example, if you own a car, your creditors cannot take it to satisfy your debt. But the dealer who sold you the car can repossess it, if he took a lien when he sold it to you. On the other hand, if you own a boat, an item not included in the list, your creditors could sue you and have the sheriff or constable take the boat and sell it to pay off the debt.

*As you can see, most of what the average person owns is exempt. This means that even if you are sued, you do not have to worry about losing your property. Of course the person who extended credit to you to buy the item will usually have a lien allowing him to take the goods back if you don't pay.*

And remember, your creditors know the law also. They know they can't force you to pay, and therefore would probably like to talk with you about finding a way to work things out.

### Can they take my wages?
### "Probably not. . ."

*Dear Mr. Alderman:*

*I owe lots of people money, but my family comes first. I buy groceries and clothing, and everything else I earn goes to pay my bills. I am worried that if I don't pay my bills soon, the creditors will take part of my wages. I couldn't even afford the basics if this happened. Can they do this?*

The Texas Constitution guarantees that a person's wages are protected from his or her creditors. Under the law there are only two groups of debts that you must be concerned with: child support and taxes. If you owe money for either of these, your wages may be attached to pay the debt. *In all other cases, your creditors may not take any of your wages.*

Remember, this is a *Texas* law. In nearly every other state a portion of your wages may be taken by any creditor to satisfy the debt. For example, if you work part-time in Texas and part-time in Oklahoma, your Oklahoma wages may be subject to your creditors.

*Best advice:* As you can tell from this letter, and the one right before it, creditors in Texas have very few legal remedies when it comes to enforcing debts. Because of this they are usually more than willing to work with you to try and arrange a fair payment plan. *If you are having trouble with your creditors, and just need some time to rearrange your debts, contact your creditors and see what you can work out. It is in everyone's best interest to try to reach a compromise.*

### Can my creditors take my IRA?
### "Not anymore!"

*Dear Mr. Alderman:*
*I recently lost my job and have fallen behind in paying my bills. I am trying to keep up, but some of my creditors want to be paid in full and have threatened to sue me. I heard you say that they can't take my wages, but I am concerned that we will lose our savings if they take our IRA. Is there any way I can protect my retirement money?*

Prior to September 1, 1987, a creditor who sued you and won in court could probably take your IRA funds to satisfy the judgment. This was an unfortunate situation because, as the previous letters show, most of your other property is exempt from your creditors. The legislature has changed this, however, by passing a law that exempts most retirement plans and IRAs from your creditors.

Under this law a qualified IRA may not be taken by your creditors, even if they go to court, sue, and win. This money is considered so important for your retirement that the state has decided to allow you to keep it. In other words, the answer to your question about protecting your money . . . keep it in the IRA. Of course, as I pointed out before, other savings, such as a simple savings account, may be taken by your creditors once they sue and win.

### Can my creditors take my wife's property?
### "Maybe not."

*Dear Mr. Alderman:*

*I have a judgment rendered against me in Harris County by a California credit card company. I have not heard from them about trying to enforce the judgment. I have no assets or funds that would be available to them if they tried to enforce it. I am now concerned because my wife may inherit a large sum of money. She is not named in the judgment. Can they try to collect against her if she inherits the money?*

As I discuss on pages 181 to 182, Texas is a "community property state." This means that most of the property owned by a husband and wife is "community." Community property may be viewed as being jointly owned. Community property, therefore, generally is subject to the debts of either of the spouses.

On the other hand, "separate property" is property that belongs to just one spouse and is not subject to the debts of the other. Separate property includes property that was owned before the marriage as well as property inherited. In your case, your wife's inheritance probably would be considered separate property and would not be subject to your debt. She should be careful not to commingle the property, or do anything to ratify your debt. If she does, the property could become subject to the debt.

### Can I stop harassing phone calls?
### "They must stop."

*Dear Mr. Alderman:*

*My creditors won't leave me alone. I know I should pay my bills, and I will as soon as I can, but I am even going to lose my job if I don't get some sleep. The most annoying thing they do is call me in the middle of the night and say things like: "I don't know how a deadbeat like you can sleep. Don't you feel guilty about not paying your bills?" I have started pulling my phone cord out at night, but as soon as I plug it in, the calls begin. How can I stop this? Do I report them to the telephone company? I have even tried changing my phone number.*

As the introduction to this chapter points out, there are two laws that protect you from harassment by debt collectors, the *Texas Debt Collection Act,* and the federal *Fair Debt Collection Practices Act.* Both laws prohibit debt collectors from harassing you over the phone.

The federal law makes it illegal for debt collectors to engage in any conduct designed to harass, oppress, or abuse you in connection with the collection of a debt. It is specifically made illegal to cause a phone to ring repeatedly with intent to annoy, abuse, or harass; to call without giving the caller's identity; or, to call after 9:00 p.m. or before 8:00 a.m. The federal law also states that once you notify the debt collector, in writing, that you want him to stop communications with you, the debt collector *must stop all communication except advising you of his next step.*

Under the Fair Debt Collection Practices Act, you can stop the debt collector from calling you and he may have already violated the law by his conduct so far. *But the Fair Debt Collection Practices Act applies only to a "debt collector," that is, someone in the business of collecting debts for another.* It doesn't apply to a creditor collecting his own debts. If the calls have been from a collection agency, the federal law applies. If the calls are directly from the store, the federal law does not apply; but the Texas law *does.*

Unlike the federal law, the Texas Debt Collection Act applies to anyone trying to collect a debt. This includes the store that sold you the goods and any agency it hires to collect the debt. Although the Texas law is not as broad as the federal law, you still can use it to prevent any further harassment. Under the Texas law, it is illegal to oppress, harass, or abuse any person in connection with the collection of a debt. The law specifically provides that a debt collector may not place phone calls without disclosing the name of the person calling; may not call with the intent to annoy or harass; and may not cause the phone to ring repeatedly or continuously with the intent to harass.

If you feel that you are being harassed, you should immediately contact the creditor and the debt collector (if they are not the same person), and tell them that you expect them to cease all further harassment. Do it in writing and mail it, certified, return-receipt-requested. You also should contact the appropriate state and federal agencies that enforce these laws. The federal law is enforced by the Federal Trade Commission, and the state law is enforced by the attorney general's office. Additionally, both of these laws let you collect substantial civil damages if you have been injured as a result of unlawful collection. If you have suffered injury, you should see a private attorney about filing a lawsuit. I should remind you that, if you are successful, you are entitled to recover your attorney's fees as well.

### Can they tell my boss?
### "You may be protected."

*Dear Mr. Alderman:*

*I owe several stores money. I just got a new job and I am paying them back as fast as I can. Most of the creditors have been very nice and have allowed me to pay as best I can, but one debt collector has told me that if I don't pay everything I owe, he will call my boss and tell him he has a deadbeat working for him. I know I will be fired if he does that. The only way I can pay this one particular store is not to pay anyone else. Is there any way to protect myself? Can they tell people that I owe them money?*

If it really is a debt collector calling you, as opposed to the store itself, then it is illegal for them to call your boss. The federal law governing debt collection, which applies only to someone trying to collect a debt owed to someone else, says that debt collectors may only communicate with other people to try to locate you. *The law expressly makes it illegal for them to call your employer and try to force him to make you pay.*

I suggest that you contact the debt collector, in writing, and demand that he stop all communication with third parties. *The federal law also provides that if you write them to stop collection efforts, they must cease all communication except to tell you that they are stopping and what they intend to do next.* If they continue, contact the Federal Trade Commission. If their action has harmed you, you may also consider seeing an attorney to bring a private lawsuit. Under the law you may be entitled to punitive damages as well as your actual loss.

*Be aware that this law does not apply to people collecting their own debts.* They are governed by the Texas law which probably lets them contact your employer, unless it is done in a harassing or abusive manner.

### My check bounced. What can they do?
### "It may be a crime."

*Dear Mr. Alderman:*

*The new dress at the department store was irresistible. The only problem was that the check I used didn't have any money to back it up. After the check bounced I told the store manager that as soon as I got paid I would pay off the check, but they insist that I pay them right away. They said that it is criminal to pay for something with a check that bounces and that, unless I paid them soon, they would turn it over to the district attorney. Can they do this? I didn't steal the dress—I plan to pay for it.*

What you have done is probably criminal under Texas law and the store has the right to turn the matter over to the district attorney, who could prosecute. *I strongly recommend that you immediately pay the store the money you owe it.*

Under Texas law the issuance of a "bad check" is a Class C misdemeanor and you could receive a fine or even be put in jail. This law states that it is illegal to give someone a check knowing that you do not have enough money in the bank to cover it. As a practical matter, if you quickly pay the check, you probably will not be prosecuted; but based on what you say in your letter, you have violated the law.

*You should be aware, however, of the difference between passing a "bad check" and stopping payment for a reason. It is not illegal to stop payment on a check when you have enough money in your account to pay it.* For example, suppose when you got the dress home, you discovered that it was damaged, so you took it back to the store. The store refused to give you back your money, even though it had a sign saying that it would give a refund if the goods were returned within 24 hours. If you stopped payment on the check, the store could not have you prosecuted under this law. If the store wanted to try to collect the money, it would have to pursue its civil remedies.

Be careful if you are thinking about stopping payment on a check to a mechanic. Read the next letter before you do.

### My check bounced. Can they repossess my car?
### "They can if the check was for repairs."

*Dear Mr. Alderman:*

*The other day I had the brakes fixed on my car. I paid the bill of $79.95 with a check. I thought I had more than enough money in the bank but apparently I didn't. The check bounced and a few days later I found my car was missing. When I called the police to report it stolen, they said it had been repossessed. I called the repo man and*

*was told that I had to pay the $79.95 plus $350 in repossession costs
to get it back. I paid and now I am mad. What are my rights?*

You have probably heard me say that, in most cases, if someone isn't paid
for what they sell you, they can't just come and take it back. They have to
go to court and sue you. Well, unfortunately for you there is one big exception to this.

A mechanic has a lien on your car whenever he repairs it. Until you
pay he does not have to give it back. And if you pay with a check that is
dishonored, or if you stop payment, the mechanic has the right to repos-
sess your car. The mechanic cannot forcefully take your car, but he can
have a repo man come out in the middle of the night and remove it. So it
looks like the mechanic does have the right to take your car back.

The harder question is what are your rights with respect to the repo
man who charged you $350 for taking the car and held it until you paid.
As of the writing of this book it looks like the repo man has the right to
keep the car until you pay, but he will be responsible if he acts unreasonably, for example, by charging an unfair price. The repo man, like anyone else who performs a service, warrants that he will perform in a good
and workmanlike manner, and under the Deceptive Trade Practices Act
he would be responsible if he charged a grossly excessive price. If you
find that the ordinary reasonable charge for this type of service is, for
example, $100, I would consider filing a claim in small claims court for a
violation of the DTPA. (See Chapter Ten.)

### How long is a judgment good for?
### "A judgment can be good forever."

*Dear Mr. Alderman:*
*In 1986 my house was foreclosed on, and I was sued. The bank got a
judgment against me. How long will this appear on my credit
report? How long is the judgment good for? I was told that the judgment is only good for ten years. Is there some period of time after
which I will no longer be obligated to pay?*

As discussed on page 4, a judgment stays on your credit report for sev-
en years. After that time it becomes obsolete and generally cannot be
reported by a credit bureau. This does not mean, however, that you don't
still owe the money. As long as there is a valid judgment against you
steps can be taken to collect. A judgment is enforceable for ten years. It

can be renewed for another ten years, however, if certain action is taken by the creditor. As long as the creditor continues to take steps to try to enforce the judgment, it can be enforced indefinitely.

### The buyer of my house didn't make his payments; how can I owe the money?
### "That is how an assumption works."

*Dear Mr. Alderman:*

*I sold my house to a buyer who assumed my existing mortgage. I have now discovered that the buyer has not paid the mortgage and has moved out of the house. The mortgage company has asked me to pay the full amount owed and to continue making payments. I don't mind picking up the future installments, but it doesn't seem fair that I have to pay the past due amounts.*

It may not seem "fair," but legally you are obligated for these payments. When a house is sold and a buyer assumes the mortgage, the buyer is simply agreeing to pay the money that the seller owes on the mortgage. The seller, however, is still obligated on the note and is responsible if the buyer doesn't make the payments. If the buyer defaults, the seller is responsible for all of the payments the buyer may have missed, as well as any future payments.

So what will happen if you do not make these payments? The mortgage company will probably foreclose on the house and sell it to pay off the note. As the next letter indicates, that may not be the end of your problems. When a buyer assumes a seller's mortgage, the seller remains legally obligated on the note. To eliminate this problem, the seller can require that the buyer arrange his own financing and pay off the seller note.

### My house was foreclosed. How can I still owe money?
### "Foreclosure does not extinguish a debt."

*Dear Mr. Alderman:*

*Several years ago we had financial problems, and our house was foreclosed. Since that time, we have been able to get back on our feet and are paying all of our bills on time. Now we have received a letter that we owe $23,000 on our house note. How is this possible? Do we have to pay this? What are our alternatives?*

Unfortunately, your letter is not the only one I have received about this problem. Many other people find themselves in the same situation. And from a legal standpoint, you owe the money.

When property is foreclosed upon, it is sold, and the proceeds are applied to the debt. If the sale price is more than what you owe, you will get money back. If the sale price is less, as was the case with your house, you still owe the difference between the sale price and the debt. You also will owe the costs of the foreclosure proceeding. In other words, you are legally responsible for the money. As a practical matter, however, you should first see if the creditor will work with you. Perhaps you can come up with a payment plan you can live with.

Because of the large amount involved, you also should consider bankruptcy. I realize that many people think of bankruptcy as a radical alternative, but it may be the best way to really get a fresh start on your finances. There are many attorneys who handle consumer bankruptcy, and specialists are listed in the yellow pages.

# CHAPTER SEVEN

# Divorce & Child Custody

THERE are few things in a person's life as traumatic as family law problems—for example, divorce. No matter who wants it, or how agreeable the parties are, divorce is always difficult to deal with. And when children are involved, divorce becomes even more complicated, both psychologically and legally.

In most cases, the parties to a divorce will be represented by an attorney, and their legal questions will be answered by that person. But knowing a little bit of law before you see an attorney can help you understand the process that is about to so seriously affect you. For example, how long should it take, what will happen, and what factors can simplify or complicate the process?

Finally, as with any other legal service that usually requires the assistance of an attorney, I strongly urge you to shop around before you hire one. Not too long ago I did a report for TV on attorneys' fees. We called nearly 30 attorneys, at random from the phone book, and asked them all what they would charge for the same basic legal service. The prices ranged from $45 to $700. The moral is simple for standardized legal services, such as a simple divorce, shop around and compare prices. You may be surprised how much money you can save.

### How long do we have to live together to have a common law marriage? "One second."

*Dear Mr. Alderman:*
*My "friend" and I have been living together for nearly six years. We are very much in love, but just don't want to be married. Last week, one of my friends told me that if we lived together for seven years we would have a common law marriage, whether we wanted it or not. This has us concerned. Should we live apart for a while? Does it matter if we put it in writing that we are not married? What can we do?*

You may not have to do anything. Just living together, for any length of time, is not enough to form a common law marriage. To have a common law marriage in Texas you must do three things: You must agree to be married, hold yourself out as married, and live together. Simply living together is not enough. Once you agree that you want to be married, and hold yourselves out as married (for example, by using the titles Mr. and Mrs.), the moment you live together you are husband and wife under Texas law. On the other hand, if you keep your separate names, and let people know you are not married, you can live together forever and probably not have a common law marriage. If you do not want to be considered married, make sure that you take all possible steps to maintain your separate identities, and let people know you are not husband and wife. If you decide to marry, I would recommend you have a civil or church ceremony just to end any doubts about your relationship.

### Is there such a thing as a common law divorce?
### "Sort of."

*Dear Mr. Alderman:*
*I lived with a man for five years. During that time, we probably were a common law husband and wife. We split up about six years ago and I assumed that I was single and free to marry again. Now I am concerned. I thought I heard you say that there is no such thing as a common law divorce. Do I have to go to court and get divorced before I remarry?*

Until recently there was no such thing as a common law divorce. If you had a common law marriage, you were married until you obtained a divorce. In 1989, however, the legislature changed the law. Now, a common law marriage must be asserted within one year after the relationship ends, or an action will be barred by law. In other words, if you do not assert the marriage within a year, there is, in effect, a common law divorce. In your case, since you split up six years ago, this law prevents either party from going to court to prove a common law marriage.

### Can I get alimony?
### "Not unless your spouse agrees."

*Dear Mr. Alderman:*
*I have been married for 15 years. Most of that time I was what you*
*would call a housewife. Of course, for me, it was a full-time job.*
*Even though we never talked about it, I think it was always under-*
*stood that my husband would pursue his career, while I gave up*
*mine to raise the family.*
*As you might have guessed, now that our child is 13, my husband*
*has left and wants a divorce. I have started looking for a job, but it*
*isn't easy and I really don't have much training. I would like to go*
*back to school and finish my degree, but I can't afford it. If we do get*
*divorced, will I be able to get some alimony to help me live and get a*
*career going?*

Unfortunately, probably not. Texas is the only state where court-ordered
alimony is not allowed. Your husband can agree to pay you alimony, and
such agreements can be enforced, but if he does not the court cannot order
it. As discussed in Chapter 18, Texas is a community property state, and
upon any dissolution of a marriage, whether by death or divorce, the property is divided in accordance with the community property rules. Alimony
is not allowed because, at least in theory, each party has taken half of what
you acquired and both spouses are going out "even."

Of course the fallacy in this rule is that both parties may not have even
capacity to continue to earn money. Because you have not worked, you
will probably earn much less than your husband and may have to spend a
good deal of time and money retraining yourself. The Texas Legislature
has considered changing the law to allow alimony in such cases, but so
far all the proposals have been defeated.

Your husband may, however, have to pay child support for your child.
Under the law, both parents are obligated to support their child. The letter
and reply on pages 66 to 73 explains how child support is computed.

### My ex-husband was supposed to pay the debts. Now they are coming after me. Can they do this?
### "A divorce decree is just between you and your spouse."

*Dear Mr. Alderman:*
*My husband and I were divorced about a year ago. In our settlement*
*he agreed to pay all the debts, including a mortgage on the house.*
*He paid some of them, but has not paid the mortgage. I should also*
*point out that he was given the house and lives there. Now the mort-*

*gage company has contacted me and wants me to pay. I sent them a copy of the divorce decree, but they said it didn't matter. How can this be? I thought my husband was legally obligated to pay? Can they really sue me if I don't pay?*

Unfortunately, the answer is probably yes. Even though your divorce decree says your husband agrees to pay the mortgage, if he does not, you are still obligated. This would be true of any debt that you incurred while you were married.

The reason is that when you incurred the debt, you and your husband entered into a contract with the creditor in which you promised to pay. When you were divorced, you entered into an agreement between you and your husband determining who would pay what. That agreement is not between you and the creditor. In effect, your husband has agreed to pay what you owe the creditor. If he does not, the creditor comes after you and then you have to go after your ex.

The bottom line is that a divorce decree only affects the relationship between the parties to the marriage. It does not release either party from existing obligations. The best way to protect against this is to make sure debts are paid in full before the divorce becomes final or get the creditor to agree in writing. If you trust your ex-spouse to pay, and he or she does not, you may end up footing the bill.

### How much child support should I get?
### "There is no set amount."

*Dear Mr. Alderman:*

*I have been married for seven years. Last month my husband left me. I have decided to file for divorce, and I was wondering how much money I could get my husband to pay for the children. He has a very good job and left me with very little. I asked him how much he would pay and he told me, "As little as I can. I will have a new family soon and I need my money." This doesn't seem fair. I think my children should get paid before his "new family." What does the law say?*

Until recently there were no set guidelines for how much money a spouse should pay in child support. The judge looked at all the facts of the case and did what he or she thought was fair. In 1989, however, the legislature enacted a law providing guidelines for awarding child support. Although the guidelines are not binding on the court, they are generally followed and should give you a good idea of how much you are entitled to.

What follows is the relevant part of this law as amended through 1993. The section numbers refer to the Texas Family Code. The material in italics was added in 1993.

## § 14.052. Guidelines for the Support of a Child

(a) Purpose. The guidelines for the support of a child in this chapter are intended to guide the courts in determining equitable amounts of child support in any suit affecting the parent-child relationship, including without limitation actions involving divorce, modification, and paternity, and in any proceeding brought under a reciprocal support act.

(b) Factors. In determining the amount of child support, the court shall be guided by the guidelines and may consider, in varying form or following the guidelines:

(1) the needs of the child;

(2) the ability of the parents to contribute to the support of the child;

(3) any financial resources available for the support of the child; and

(4) the amount of possession of and access to a child.

## § 14.053. Establishing any Order of Child Support

(a) Order Based on Guidelines. An order of child support shall be based on the "net resources" of the obligor and obligee, which shall be considered by the court, together with the other factors listed in the guidelines for the support of a child in this chapter. Whenever feasible, gross income should first be computed on an annual basis and then should be recalculated to determine average monthly gross income.

(b) Net Resources Defined. "Net resources," for the purpose of determining child support liability, are 100 percent of all wage and salary income and other compensation for personal services (including commissions, overtime pay, tips and bonuses), interest, dividends, royalty income, self-employment income (as described in Subsection (c) of this section), net rental income (defined as rent after deducting operating expenses and mortgage payments, but not including noncash items such as depreciation), and all other income actually being received, including but not limited to severance pay, retirement benefits, pensions, trust income, annuities, capital gains, social security benefits, unemployment benefits, disability and workers' compensation benefits, interest, income from notes but not including return of principal or capital, accounts receivable regardless of the source, gifts and prizes, spousal maintenance, and alimony, less (subtracting) 100 percent of social security taxes, federal income tax withholding for a single person claiming one personal exemption and the standard deduction, union dues, and expense for health insurance coverage for the obligor's child. Benefits paid pursuant to aid for families with dependent children and any other child support received from any source shall be disregarded in calculating net resources.

(c) Self-Employment Income. Income from self-employment, whether positive or negative, includes benefits allocated to an individual from a business or undertaking in the form of a proprietorship, partnership, joint venture, close corporation, agency, or independent contractor, less ordinary and necessary expenses required to produce that income, but may exclude amounts allowable under federal income tax law as depreciation, tax credits, or any other business expenses shown by the evidence to be inappropriate to the determination of income for the purpose of calculating child support.

(d) Health Insurance. The guidelines for a court order for the support of a child in this chapter assume that the court will order the obligor to provide health insurance coverage for the child subject of the suit in addition to the amount of child support, calculated pursuant to these guidelines. If the court finds and sets forth in the order setting child support that the obligee will maintain health insurance coverage at the obligee's expense for the child, the court may increase the amount of child support to be paid by the obligor in an amount not exceeding the total expense to the oblig_e for maintaining health insurance coverage. *As additional child support, the court shall allocate between the parties, according to the parties' circumstances, the reasonable and necessary health care expenses of a child that are not reimbursed by health insurance.*

(e) Additional Factors. The court may consider any additional factors that increase or decrease the ability of the obligor to make child support payments. When appropriate, in order to determine the "net resources" available for child support the court may assign a reasonable amount of "income" attributable to assets that do not currently produce income. However, the court shall consider whether certain nonincome-producing property can be liquidated without an unreasonable financial sacrifice because of cyclical or other market conditions. If there is not an effective market for the property, the carrying costs of such an investment, including property taxes and note payments, shall be offset against the income attributed to the property. The court may also assign a reasonable amount of "income" to income-producing assets that have been voluntarily transferred or reduced in earnings with the effect of reducing the net resources of the party. As used in this section, "property" and "assets" include both real and personal property and assets, including a business and investments.

(f) Intentional Unemployment or Underemployment. If the actual income of the obligor is significantly less than what the obligor could earn because the obligor is intentionally unemployed or underemployed, the court may apply these guidelines to the earning potential of the obligor.

(g) Furnish Information. The court shall require the parties to furnish sufficient information to enable it to accurately identify the parties' net resources and their abilities to provide child support. The court should request copies of the last two years' tax returns, accompanied by financial statements of the parties, and current wage status.

(h) Computing Net Monthly Income. To assist the courts in establishing the amount of a child support order, the agency charged with enforcing child support orders under Part D of Title IV of the federal Social Security Act (42 U.S.C. Section 651 et seq.) shall annually promulgate tax charts to compute "net monthly income," subtracting from gross income social security taxes and federal income tax withholding for a single person claiming one personal exemption and the standard deduction.

(i) Equal Application. These guidelines shall be applied without regard to the sex of the obligor, obligee, or the child.

(j) Agreements. This section does not prohibit the parties from agreeing to an amount of child support that varies from the guidelines or prohibit the court from approving the agreement concerning support of the child as provided by Section 14.06 of this code.

(k) Wage or Salary Presumption. In the absence of sufficient evidence to determine the wages and salary income of the obligor or obligee it shall be presumed that the obligor or obligee has wages or salary equal to the prevailing federal minimum wage for a 40-hour week.

(l) *Retroactive Support. The guidelines for the support of a child in this chapter are intended to guide the court in determining the amount of retroactive child support that may be ordered under this chapter or Chapter 13 of this code. In ordering retroactive child support, the court shall consider the net resources of the obligor during the relevant time period.*

## § 14.054. Evidentiary Factors

In applying the guidelines for the support of a child in this chapter, the court shall be guided by the guidelines for the support of a child in this chapter. However, the court may, in rendering its final determination of the amount of support, set the amount of child support either within or outside the range recommended in Section 14.055 of this code if relevant factors other than the guidelines justify a variance from the guidelines. In making its final determination, the court shall consider all relevant factors, including but not limited to:

(1) the amount of the obligee's net resources, including the earning potential of the obligee if the actual income of the obligee is significantly less than what the obligee could earn because the obligee is intentionally unemployed or underemployed and including, as provided by Section 14.053(e) of this code, any increase or decrease in the income of the obligee or income that may be attributed to the property and assets of the obligee:

(2) the age and needs of the child;

(3) child care expenses incurred by either party in order to maintain gainful employment;

(4) whether either party has the managing conservatorship or actual physical custody of another child;

(5) the amount of child support actually and currently being paid or received by either party under another child support order;

(6) the amount of alimony or spousal maintenance actually and currently being paid or received by a party;

(7) the expenses for a son or daughter for education beyond secondary school;

(8) whether the obligor or obligee has an automobile, housing, or other benefits furnished by his or her employer, another person, or a business entity;

(9) the amount of other deductions from the wage or salary income and from other compensation for personal services of the parties;

(10) provision for health care insurance and payment of uninsured medical expenses;

(11) special or extraordinary educational, health care, or other expenses of the parties or of the child;

(12) the cost of travel in order to exercise access to or possession of a child;

(13) positive or negative cash flow from any real and personal property and assets, including a business and investments;

(14) debts or debt service assumed by either party; and

(15) any other reason or reasons consistent with the best interest of the child, taking into consideration the circumstances of the parents.

## § 14.055 Guidelines: Amount Ordered

(a) Rebuttable Presumption. The guidelines for the support of a child in this chapter are specifically designed to apply to situations in which the obligor's monthly net resources are *$6,000* or less. In any suit affecting the parent-child relationship, there is a rebuttable presumption that an order containing the amount of periodic child support payments established by the schedule provided in this section is reasonable and that the order is in the best interest of the child. A court may determine that the application of the guidelines would be unjust or inappropriate under the circumstances.

(b) Schedule: *$6,000* or Less Monthly Net Resources. In rendering an order of child support under circumstances in which the obligor's monthly net resources are $6,000 or less, the court shall presumptively apply the following schedule:

CHILD SUPPORT GUIDELINES
BASED ON THE MONTHLY NET RESOURCES OF THE OBLIGOR

| | |
|---|---|
| 1 child | 20% of Obligor's Net Resources |
| 2 children | 25% of Obligor's Net Resources |

| | |
|---|---|
| 3 children | 30% of Obligor's Net Resources |
| 4 children | 35% of Obligor's Net Resources |
| 5 children | *40% of Obligor's Net Resources* |
| *6+ children* | *Not less than the amount for 5 children* |

(c) More Than *$6,000* Monthly Net Resources. In situations in which the obligor's net resources exceed *$6,000* per month, the court shall presumptively apply the percentage guidelines in Subsection 9b of this section to the first *$6,000* of the obligor's net resources. Without further reference to the percentage recommended by these guidelines, the court may order additional amounts of child support as *appropriate* depending on the *income of the parties and the proven* needs of the children. *The proper calculation of a child support order that exceeds the presumptive amount established for the first $6,000 of the obligor's net resources requires that the entire amount of the presumptive award be subtracted from the proven total needs of the child. After the presumptive award is subtracted, the court shall allocate between the parties the responsibility to meet the additional needs of the child according to the circumstances of the parties. However, in no event may the obligor be required to pay more than an amount equal to 100 percent of the proven needs of the child as child support.*

(d) Partial Termination of Support Obligation. A child support order that provides for the termination of the support for one child because the child reaches the age of majority, graduates from high school, or for some other reason, but continues the support order for another child must establish a level of support for the remaining child or children in accordance with these guidelines.

(e) Temporary Orders. The rebuttable presumption established in this section is applicable to temporary orders for the support of a child. This subsection does not impair the authority of the court to enter other temporary orders under this code.

## § 14.056. Modification of Prior Orders

(a) Effect of Guidelines. The court may consider the guidelines for the support of a child in this chapter to determine whether there has been a material and substantial change in circumstances under Section 14.08(c)(2) of this code that may warrant a modification of an existing child support order if the modification is in the best interest of the child. However, an increase in the needs, standard of living, or lifestyle of the obligee since the rendering of the existing order does not warrant an increase in the obligor's child support obligation. If the amount of support of a child contained in the order sought to be modified is not in substantial compliance with the guidelines, this may warrant a modification of a prior order in accordance with the guidelines if the modification is in the best interest of the child.

(b) Additional Factors. In addition to the factors listed in these guidelines, a court may consider other relevant factors. The support obligation owed to a subsequently born or adopted child does not constitute cause to decrease the amount of an existing child support order. The history of support voluntarily provided in excess of the court order does not constitute cause to increase the amount of an existing child support order.

(c) Net Resources of New Spouse. A court may not add any portion of the net resources of a new spouse to the net resources of an obligor or obligee in order to calculate the amount of child support to be ordered on a motion to modify. Similarly, a court may not subtract the needs of a new spouse or of a dependent of a new spouse from the net resources of the obligor or obligee. An increase in the needs, standard of living, or lifestyle of the obligee does not constitute cause to increase the obligor's child support obligation.

### Do I need an attorney to file for divorce?
### "No, but it sure can make life simpler."

*Dear Mr. Alderman:*
*My wife and I have decided that our brief attempt at marriage isn't going to work. We know Texas is a "no-fault" divorce state, so there wouldn't be any trouble getting a divorce, but we don't have a lot of extra money and can't afford to spend a fortune on attorney's fees. We have no children, and agree on how everything should be split. Is it legal to do your own divorce, and do you think we could handle it ourselves?*

Anyone can represent themselves in court. Whether you should do it is another question. Even though a simple divorce is not complicated, any attempt at practicing law by a layperson can be difficult and there are many traps for the amateur to fall into. There are, however, several books on the market that help take you step-by-step through the divorce. You may want to look at them and see if you think you could do it.

As far as I am concerned, a better approach is to shop around and find an attorney that will handle your divorce inexpensively. There are many competent attorneys who will do simple divorces for a few hundred dollars in attorneys' fees. I realize this is still more than it will cost to just buy the book and do it yourself, but with an attorney you are assured that it will be done properly and you may save enough time to make it worth your while. Again, the important thing is to shop around and get prices from several lawyers before you make a selection.

### Do I have to live in Texas to get divorced there?
### "Yes!"

*Dear Mr. Alderman:*
*I am in the process of relocating to Texas. I am coming without my wife. We have decided to get a divorce but neither of us has seen a lawyer or filed any papers. I will not be living in Texas until two months from now but I would like to get things going on the divorce. Can I file in Texas now?*

No. To file for divorce the court you file with has to have what is called "jurisdiction." This is a legal term meaning that the court has the power to hear the case and make a decision. In the case of a divorce, a court only has jurisdiction if you have been a domiciliary of this state for the preceding six months, and a resident of the county where you file for the preceding ninety days. In other words, if you want to get a divorce in Texas you will have to wait until you have made Texas your permanent home for six months. Then you file where you have lived for the past 90 days. If you want a divorce sooner than that you will probably have to file in the state where you presently live.

### How can I get my husband to pay child support?
### "He may be thrown in jail."

*Dear Mr. Alderman:*
*I have been divorced for five years. I have two children, ages 7 and 9. My husband is supposed to pay child support each month, but for*

*the last three months he has not paid. He says that he has too many other bills and can't afford it. I know he has other obligations, but I need the money to support the kids. What can I do?*

Unlike most debts, child support obligations are very enforceable in Texas. If a person doesn't pay as ordered, his wages can be garnisheed (taken by the court) or, in some cases, he can even be thrown in jail until he pays. All of this, however, will have to be done through the courts, usually with the assistance of an attorney.

You may want to talk with the attorney who handled your divorce and ask him or her for assistance. Another alternative is to contact the Child Support Enforcement Division of the Texas Attorney General's Office, 1-800-252-3515. Their job is to assist in the enforcement of child support obligations. Usually, once your husband understands the consequences of not paying, he will begin to do so.

## What must I show to get a divorce?
### "Just that you don't get along."

*Dear Mr. Alderman:*

*My husband and I have had problems for several years. We seem to do nothing but fight. Finally, we have decided that we just are not right for each other and that we should get a divorce. No one in my family has ever been divorced and we don't know much about it. Our first question is, what do we have to prove to end our marriage? Do I have to say he committed adultery or beat me?*

Not any more. It used to be that to get a divorce it was necessary to show cruelty, adultery, abandonment, or that you had lived apart for three years. This is no longer necessary. The law now allows the court to grant a divorce if you show:

that the marriage has become insupportable because of discord or conflict of personalities that destroys the legitimate ends of the marriage relationship and prevents any reasonable expectations of reconciliation.

What this legalese means is that Texas is now a "no-fault" divorce state. You can get a divorce simply by showing that you no longer get along. It is not necessary to prove that either party did anything wrong or to explain why it is that you can't remain married. In fact, if one party doesn't want to be married and the other does, this difference alone would be enough for the court to grant the divorce.

### I just got divorced. When can I remarry?
### "In thirty days."

*Dear Mr. Alderman:*
*My divorce was finalized last year. My husband and I have been liv-*
*ing apart for more than two years and I have been seeing another*
*man for almost a year. He wants to get married but says that you*
*have to wait a year after a divorce. I want to get married right now.*
*Do I have to wait a year?*

No. Under Texas law you may remarry 30 days following the day your divorce is decreed. In fact, in some cases you can marry even sooner. For example, if you wanted to remarry your husband there is no waiting period. Also, in special circumstances, a court may waive the 30 days prohibition if requested. In other words, if he really wants to marry you, the most you should have to wait is 30 days.

### How do I find my adopted child?
### "There may be help available if he wants to be found."

*Dear Mr. Alderman:*
*Many years ago I placed my son for adoption. I have no regrets and*
*still believe it was the right thing to do. Now, however, I am curious*
*how things turned out, and what kind of a person he is. Is there any*
*way for me to find out who adopted my son?*

Although it is generally very difficult to find out who adopted your child, it may be possible if the child also wants to contact you. The Texas Department of Protective and Regulatory Services maintains a Voluntary Adoption Registry. This is a system that allows adopted children, birth parents, and biological siblings to locate each other if they wish. To get more information about the Registry, contact:

Central Adoption Registry
Texas Department of Protective and Regulatory Services
MC Y-943
P.O. Box 149030
Austin, Texas 78714-9030
(512) 502-3185

# CHAPTER EIGHT

# Door-to-Door Sales

**T**RADITIONALLY, there are few salespeople as persuasive as those who travel door-to-door. We have all heard stories of the person who bought the high-priced vacuum cleaner or the set of encyclopedias from the smooth-talking, fast-moving traveling salesman only to discover later that the price was too high, or the goods unnecessary.

But door-to-door selling does provide a good alternative for people who are unable to go out and shop, or who, because of their obligations at home, must remain at home during the day. It is convenient and practical for many of us to shop at home.

So how do we balance the problems of high-pressure selling with the convenience of home sales? The answer reached by both Congress and the Texas legislature is the same: Pass a law that requires that door-to-door salespeople give you a chance to change your mind. In Texas this law is called the **Home Solicitation Sales Act.**

**The books seemed like a good idea,
but now I don't want them . . .
Help!
"Door-to-door sales give you time to change your mind."**

*Dear Mr. Alderman:*

*The other day I was sitting at home when the doorbell rang. A nice-looking man, well dressed, asked if he could come in and talk to me about a program that could help my kids in school. I said OK, and after about an hour I agreed to buy the complete set of books. He promised that it would help my kids in school and that it was approved by the school board. Right after he left I talked with my neighbor and found out that what he said was true, but the school library would loan the books to my kids for free. I really don't want the books. What can I do? He was so nice and persuasive that I couldn't say no. I guess I learned a lesson: "Don't talk to door-to-door salesmen."*

You may not have learned the lesson you think. The lesson you should have learned is that *under the law you have three days to change your mind and get out of a contract entered into in your home.* Both Texas and federal law provide that a door-to-door merchant must give you a three-day cooling-off period to change your mind. Based on what you say in your letter, I believe the salesman has violated the law and you should be able to cancel the sale and not have to pay.

So what should you do? If you paid by cash you may have a problem. Try to get in touch with the company and demand your money back. If you don't get it back you can go to small claims court. If you paid by check, go to the bank at once and stop payment. If the check has already been cashed, you are in the same position as if you paid cash. If you used a credit card, contact the company and tell them you are not paying the bill and explain why. The credit card company stands in the shoes of the merchant and can't collect because the merchant has violated the law.

If you don't get your money back, contact the district attorney's office and the attorney general's office and report the company and the salesperson. You can also take steps to recover your money and if you are successful in court you can recover under the Deceptive Trade Practices Act because any violation of the Home Solicitation Sales Act is automatically a violation of the Deceptive Trade Practices Act. Look over Chapter Ten and you will see how to get substantial damages.

*Be careful when dealing with door-to-door salesmen and don't pay cash or with a check unless you are absolutely sure you want the goods. And remember, under the law all door-to-door contracts must have the following printed on them:*

---

NOTICE OF CANCELLATION

<u>(enter date of transaction)</u>

You may cancel this transaction, without any penalty or obligation, within three business days from the above date.

If you cancel, any property traded in, any payments made by you under the contract or sale, and any negotiable instrument executed by you will be returned within 10 business days following receipt by the merchant of your cancellation notice, and any security interest arising out of the transaction will be canceled.

---

*(notice continued on next page)*

If you cancel, you must make available to the merchant at your residence, in substantially as good condition as when received, any goods delivered to you under this contract or sale; or you may if you wish, comply with the instructions of the merchant regarding the return shipment of the goods at the merchant's expense and risk.

If you do not agree to return the goods to the merchant or if the merchant does not pick them up within 20 days of the date of your notice of cancellation, you may retain or dispose of the goods without any further obligation.

To cancel this transaction, mail or deliver a signed and dated copy of this cancellation notice or any other written notice, or send a telegram, to (Name of merchant), at (Address of merchant's place of business) not later than midnight of (Date).

I hereby cancel this transaction.

(Date)

(Buyer's signature)

# CHAPTER NINE

# Employment

**F**OR most of us there is nothing more important to our economic well-being than keeping a job. Those of you who have lost a job know how devastating it is and those who have not can imagine what it would be like. Unfortunately, times have been hard in Texas lately, and more and more people have begun to write with questions about their jobs, such as "when and how can I be fired?" and "what are my rights if I am?" Unfortunately, as you will see, Texas is not an employee state.

### I don't have a contract. When can I be fired?
### "Probably whenever the boss wants."

*Dear Mr. Alderman:*

*I have been working at the same job for nearly two years. I have never had a contract and really didn't think I needed one. It is a small company and everyone has always trusted everyone else to be fair. Recently, one of my friends came into work and was told "go home, you're fired." As far as I know he was doing a good job and there was no reason to fire him. I think the company has just decided they can get along without him. Now I am afraid I am next. What are my rights? Am I safe as long as I do my job well and don't violate any company rules?*

Not necessarily. Texas is basically an "employment at will" state. This means that you can be fired at will, or you can quit at will. Unless you have a contract or a union agreement, the company can fire you with no notice, and for no reason at all. The other side of that coin is that you can quit the same way. Although many states have changed this doctrine, the employment at will doctrine governs in Texas, at least for right now. I should point out, though, that this rule is not absolute. The Texas Supreme Court has found at least one exception (you can't be fired for failing to perform an illegal act) and it may be willing to find others. Also, a contract may be found many ways, and you may have an implied or oral contract with the company that would prohibit them from firing you without cause. Generally, however, you can be fired just because the company doesn't want you there.

One final point must be mentioned. In all cases, laws can change and it is important that you check to make sure the advice I give you is up to date. In the case of employment law, though, it is even more important you do so because this is a rapidly changing area of law. If a problem arises you may want to contact an attorney to make sure there hasn't been a recent development in this area.

### I think I was fired because of my age. Isn't there a law? "The law prohibits certain discrimination."

*Dear Mr. Alderman:*

*I am 62 years old, and while I don't think that is very old my boss does. She is only 34 and thinks I am too old to be dealing with customers. She recently told me to work in the stock room or quit. I do my job well and the only reason she wants me in the back is because of her "image" of the store. Is this legal? I have worked hard all my life and it doesn't seem fair.*

It doesn't seem fair, and it doesn't seem legal. Under federal law it is illegal to discriminate on the basis of age against anyone over the age of 39. The major exception to this is when the employer can establish that for the particular task age is a legitimate qualification. In your case it doesn't sound like that is the case.

If you feel that you are being discriminated against because of your age you should contact the Equal Employment Opportunity Commission, 1-800-669-3362.

### Can I be forced to take a drug test? "Probably."

*Dear Mr. Alderman:*

*I work at a small company that manufactures parts used in engines. My job is to box the finished product and in the six years I have worked here I have never had any problems performing my job well. I know this may not sound too good, but the job is so simple, I could do it in my sleep, or drunk (which I may have been on occasion.) Last week the company said that everyone had to take a drug test. If we refused we would be fired. Is this legal? I don't use drugs, but it doesn't seem fair. Don't I have some kind of constitutional right not to have to take this test?*

As of right now, a private employer in Texas probably has the right to force employees to take a drug test, and fire them if they don't. This is the result of the "employment at will" doctrine discussed in the first letter. Since you can be fired without a reason, it follows that you can also be fired for nearly any reason—including your refusal to take the test. This issue is in the courts, however, and Congress is also looking at preventing this kind of drug testing. But as of right now, you may want to take the test or risk losing your job.

The same rule would not apply, however, if you were employed by a public employer, such as the post office, or state motor vehicle department. In the case of a public or governmental employer, the constitutional right of privacy protects you. Drug testing can usually only be done under certain limited circumstances. Without getting too detailed, governmental entities may only drug test if they can justify who is going to be tested (i.e., is it someone who will endanger himself or others if impaired); when the testing is done (i.e., was there a reasonable suspicion the person may have been using drugs); how the tests were performed (i.e., was the most accurate test used); and what was done with the result (i.e., testing will be authorized more readily if the person is rehabilitated, not fired).

## Can I be forced to take a lie detector test?
## "Probably not."

*Dear Mr. Alderman:*
*I recently applied for a job and was asked to take a lie detector test. I refused and was told to look elsewhere. I don't have anything to hide, but I just don't trust these things. Is this a common practice? Do I have any legal rights?*

What happened to you is probably illegal. Under a recent federal law, it is basically illegal for an employer to ask an employee or prospective employee to take a lie detector test. It is also illegal to refuse to hire or fire someone because he or she refused to take the test. The law provides for both criminal and civil penalties for an employer who violates the law.

There is, however, a limited exception to this law. An employee may be asked to submit to a lie detector test if it is part of an ongoing investigation regarding economic loss or theft to the employer. If the employer has a reasonable suspicion that an employee was involved, a lie detector test may be given. The only other exception is with respect to government entities. They are not subject to this law.

This law is enforced by the secretary of labor and can be used by individuals in private lawsuits. I suggest you either file a complaint with the secretary of labor's office or consider a private lawsuit if you feel you have been harmed as a result of what may be an illegal practice.

### The union negotiates my contract, but I am not a member. Isn't Texas a right-to-work state? "It is, but the union still negotiates your contract."

*Dear Mr. Alderman:*

*I work for a medium-size company in West Texas. About two years ago, there was a vote in the company about joining a union. I voted no and did not join. Most of the employees voted yes. I was told that because Texas is a right-to-work state, I would not have to join the union and would not have to pay dues.*

*Last week, the union, which I did not join, voted to agree to reduce the number of overtime hours employees are allowed to work. The company has agreed. Now, I am losing money. How can this happen? How can a union I don't even belong to make contracts for me? What happened to my right to work?*

In a right-to-work state, an employee does not have to join a union or pay union dues as a condition of employment. Right-to-work means the right to work without joining a union. Nevertheless, if a majority of the employees vote to be represented by a union, then the union is the exclusive bargaining representative of all the employees, even those employees who are not members or who voted against union representation. Likewise, the union has a duty to represent, in contract negotiations and grievances, the interests of all employees. This is sometimes referred to as "majority rule with minority rights." The bottom line is that the union negotiates for you even though you are not a member.

### I work with chemicals. Do I have a right to know what they are?
### "Probably yes."

*Dear Mr. Alderman:*
*I work for a small company that cleans ships. In the course of my employment I use a chemical that is supplied to me in an unmarked drum. I have been told to always wear gloves and be careful not to spill it on me.*
*I never really thought about what was in the drum until I went to the doctor and he asked if I have been working with any dangerous chemicals. I told him I didn't know and he said, "Find out." When I asked my boss what was in the drum he said, "Don't worry, just wear gloves and be careful." I tried to push for an answer but he got mad. How can I find out what is in the drum? I am afraid I will be fired if I insist on knowing.*

Under the Occupational Safety Health Act (OSHA) an employer has a duty to disclose to employees if they are working with hazardous chemicals. This law, enforced by the Department of Labor, has a list of dangerous chemicals and, if you are working with any of these chemicals, you must be told. On the other hand, if the substance you are working with is not on the list, your employer has no duty to tell you.

Your employer's actions in not telling you indicate one of two things. Either the chemical you are working with is not on the list and is probably not dangerous, or he is violating the law. If you are still concerned, I suggest you contact the Department of Labor and ask them to investigate. You also should know that the law protects you if you are fired for trying to find out. An employer can't just fire employees who insist on their legal rights.

### I just quit. Can my former boss stop me from going into
### business for myself?
### "Perhaps."

*Dear Mr. Alderman:*
*For the past five years, I have been in the sales business. I am no longer satisfied working for a large company and want to go to work for a smaller one where I have more of a future. Because my back-*

*ground is basically in one field, the companies I am interested in are all in competition with my present employer.*

*I have been told that if I leave, I will not be able to work for any competing company in the southwestern states. My employer told me that my contract has a "covenant not to compete" clause that prevents me from working for someone else. Can this be true? I thought I had the right to work for whomever I wanted. Can I be prevented from earning a living?*

I cannot give you a specific answer to your question because it will depend on what your contract says and all of the facts surrounding your employment. I can tell you that there are such things as "covenants not to compete" and they are enforceable.

Under Texas law, an employer has the right to enter into an agreement with an employee that prevents the employee from competing with the employer after the employee terminates employment. Because of the harshness of such clauses, they are only enforceable if they are reasonable. This means that the geographical area and scope of the limitation must not be overbroad. The test is a balance between the employer's right to be protected against unreasonable competition from a former employee and the employee's right to work. Based on what you say in your letter, the clause may be unreasonable because it prohibits you from working within a very broad geographic area. Usually, the area limited is much smaller. For the clause to be enforceable, your employer would also have to show that, due to the nature of the business and the knowledge you obtained while working for the employer, the restriction is reasonable. If a lawsuit were to develop, the court would have the right to limit the clause to a reasonable geographic area.

Generally, the courts do not favor covenants not to compete. They do, however, serve a legitimate purpose when applied to situations where employees receive special training and knowledge that could be used in a competitive way against the employer. In these cases, the law enforces such agreements as long as they are "reasonable."

### Am I entitled to a leave if I have a child?
### "You may be."

*Dear Mr. Alderman:*
*I am three months pregnant. I recently told my employer that I would need some time off when the child was born. He told me I could have*

*a few weeks maximum. I thought it was the law that I had to be given three months leave?*

Effective August 5, 1993, the Family and Medical Leave Act generally provides that eligible employees may take family or medical leave for up to 12 weeks during any 12-month period. Unpaid leave may be taken for any of the following reasons: (1) birth of a child; (2) adoption of a child or placement of a foster child; (3) to care for a child, spouse, or parent with a serious health condition; or (4) due to the employee's own serious health condition. Upon termination of the leave, you must be reinstated to the same or an equivalent position. Your employer must also maintain health coverage during the leave period just as though you had continued working.

To be eligible to take a leave, you must satisfy two requirements. First, you must have been employed for at least one year. Second, you must have worked at least 1,250 hours during the previous 12-month period. In other words, even some part-time employees are protected by this law.

This law, however, does not apply to all employers. Because of the burden this law could place on small employers, it is limited to larger employers. The law applies only to employers with 50 or more employees for each working day during 20 or more workweeks in the current or preceding calendar year. Both part-time and full-time employees count for purposes of meeting this requirement.

If you think you are protected by this law, you should speak with your employer. If you still cannot resolve the problem, you can either consult a private attorney about a civil lawsuit, or complain to the Secretary of Labor. This is the government office that enforces the Family and Medical Leave Act.

# CHAPTER TEN

# False & Deceptive Acts

TEXAS has a law that every consumer should know by name, and that law is the **Texas Deceptive Trade Practices Act.** This is one of the most powerful consumer protection laws in the country. But, as you will see, it covers a lot more than you might think. Nearly every transaction you make, from buying a house to selling a toaster at a garage sale, falls within the scope of this law.

The Deceptive Trade Practices Act lists 24 things considered to be false, misleading, or deceptive. *And unlawful.* Basically, anything that someone does that has the potential to deceive you is prohibited by the law; and, more importantly, the law is a *no-fault* statute.

No-fault means that, in most cases, you don't have to intend to violate the law—or even know you are violating the law—to be held responsible. For example, someone thinks a car is in excellent shape and, without any intent to hurt you, says "this car is in excellent condition." If it turns out that the car was in poor condition, the seller is liable under this law. It doesn't matter that the seller had no idea that there was anything wrong with the car.

### What is the Deceptive Trade Practices Act?
### "The consumer's best friend."

*Dear Mr. Alderman:*
*I have watched you on television and you always talk about some great law that helps consumers. I think it is a "deceptive practices" law. Could you please tell me about this law and what it covers?*

The Texas Deceptive Trade Practices Act is one of the most powerful consumer protection laws in the country. *Anyone who violates the Deceptive Trade Practices Act may be liable for three times your damages, plus all your court costs and attorney's fees.* The following list identifies all the things that are made unlawful under this law. The list may sound a bit technical, but that is merely because I have used the same language the law uses.

1. Passing of goods or services as those of another;
2. Causing confusion or misunderstanding as to the source, sponsorship, approval, or certification of goods or services;
3. Causing confusion or misunderstanding as to affiliation, connection or association with, or certification by, another;
4. Using deceptive representations or designations of geographic origin in connection with goods or services;
5. Representing that goods or services have sponsorship, approval, characteristics, ingredients, uses, benefits, or quantities that they do not have, or that a person has a sponsorship, approval, status, affiliation, or connection which he does not;
6. Representing that goods are original or new if they are deteriorated, reconditioned, reclaimed, used, or second-hand;
7. Representing that goods or services are of a particular standard, quality, or grade, or that goods are of a particular style or model, if they are of another;
8. Disparaging the goods, services, or business of another by false or misleading representation of facts;
9. Advertising goods or services with intent not to sell them as advertised;
10. Advertising goods or services with intent not to supply a reasonable, expectable public demand, unless the advertisements disclosed a limitation of quantity;
11. Making false or misleading statements of fact concerning the reasons for, existence of, or amount of price reductions;
12. Representing that an agreement confers or involves rights, remedies, or obligations which it does not have or involve, or which are prohibited by law;
13. Knowingly making false or misleading statements of fact concerning the need for parts, replacement, or repair service;
14. Misrepresenting the authority of a salesman, representative, or agent to negotiate the final terms of a consumer transaction;
15. Basing a charge for the repair of any item, in whole or in part, on a guaranty or warranty instead of on the value of the actual repairs made, or work to be performed on the item, without stating, separately, the charges for the work and the charge for the warranty or guaranty, if any;

16. Disconnecting, turning back, or resetting the odometer of any motor vehicle so as to reduce the number of miles indicated on the odometer gauge;

17. Advertising of any sale by fraudulently representing that a person is going out of business;

18. Using or employing a chain-referral sales plan in connection with the sale or offer to sell of goods, merchandise, or anything of value which uses the sale's technique, plan, arrangement, or agreement in which the buyer or prospective buyer is offered the opportunity to purchase merchandise or goods and, in connection with the purchase, receives the seller's promise or representation that the buyer shall have the right to receive compensation or consideration, in any form, for furnishing to the seller the names of other prospective buyers, if receipt of the compensation or consideration is contingent upon the occurrence of an event subsequent to the time the buyer purchases the merchandise or goods;

19. Representing that a guaranty or warranty confers or involves rights or remedies, which it does not have or involve, provided, however, that nothing in this subchapter shall be construed to expand the implied warranty of merchantability, as defined in Sections 2.314 through 2.318 of the Business & Commerce Code to involve obligations in excess of those which are appropriate to the goods;

20. Selling or offering-to-sell, either directly or associated with the sale of goods or services, a right of participation in a multilevel distributorship. As used herein, "multilevel distributorship" means a sales plan for the distribution of goods or services in which promises of rebate or payment are made to individuals, conditioned upon those individuals recommending or securing additional individuals to assume positions in the sales operation, and where the rebate or payment is not exclusively conditioned on, or in relation to proceeds from the retail sales of goods;

21. Representing that work or services have been performed on, or parts replaced in, goods when the work or services were not performed or the parts not replaced;

22. Filing suit, founded upon a written contractual obligation of and signed by the defendant, to pay money arising out of or based on a consumer transaction for goods, services, loans, or extensions of credit intended primarily for personal, family, household, or agricultural use in any county other than in the county in which the defendant resides at the time of the commencement of the action or

in the county in which the defendant in fact signed the contract; provided, however, that a violation of this subsection shall not occur where it is shown by the person filing such suit he neither knew nor had reason to know that the county in which such suit was filed was neither the county in which the defendant resides at the commencement of the suit, nor the county in which the defendant in fact signed the contract; or

23. The failure to disclose information concerning goods or services that was known at the time of the transaction if such failure to disclose such information was intended to induce the consumer into a transaction into which the consumer would not have entered had the information been disclosed.

24. Using the term "incorporation," "incorporated," or an abbreviation of either of these terms in the name of a business entity that is not incorporated under the [laws of a state].

*As stated before—anyone who does any of these 24 things has violated the law, and you may have the right to recover substantial damages. But don't count on having to sue everyone. Once "they" know that "you" know about this law, you will be amazed at how cooperative some folks can become—and how quickly you can settle your dispute.*

To find out who the law applies to and how to use it, read on.

### Who can use the Deceptive Trade Practices Act?
### "Nearly everyone."

*Dear Mr. Alderman:*
*I own a small business called Bob's Repair Shop. I run the business part-time out of my garage, repairing lawn-mower motors and other small engines. The other day I bought some replacement parts from a dealer who told me the parts were just as good as the ones I usually buy. They weren't . . . and, as a result, three engines I fixed needed extensive repairs. I believe what the salesman told me wasn't true— the parts were nowhere near good as new. I want to know: Can I use the Deceptive Trade Practices Act to sue?*

You surely can! The act applies to any "consumer," and the term is defined to include any individual, partnership, corporation, or governmental entity. The only exception is a business consumer with more than $25 million in assets. I assume from your letter that you are running your business as a sole proprietorship and, therefore, you would sue as an individual. If it is a partnership or corporation, you can still use this law, but you will have to sue in the name of your business.

The other requirement of the law is that you must have purchased (or tried to purchase) goods or services. This obviously applies to you—as you bought parts from the dealer. About the only time the law doesn't apply is in the event a person makes representations in connection with free gifts. For example: If the local burger restaurant had a promotion and promised you could win a new car, free, and that car was, in fact, not new, you could not sue under this law, as you did not try to purchase the car—it was a gift.

Depending on how much money is involved, you may not need a lawyer. You can represent yourself in small claims court if your damages are less than $5,000. To find out the procedures you should use to sue under the Deceptive Trade Practices Act, read the next few letters. As you will see, the act is easy to use. *Just be sure to read the letter on page 104 and give the 60 days' notice required under the law.*

## To whom does this act apply?
## "Nearly everyone."

*Dear Mr. Alderman:*
*I just bought a stereo for $150 from someone at a garage sale. When I looked at it, the girl told me it was less than a year old and in good condition. It turns out that it is three years old and needs a lot of work. Does the Texas law about false statements apply here, and can I get three times my damages?*

Under the Texas Deceptive Trade Practices Act, you can sue anyone, including an individual not in business, if he or she violates the law. In your case, making a false representation about the stereo violates the law. If you can prove the statement was made and was false, you would be entitled to three times your damages. In this case, your damages are the difference between the value of a one-year-old stereo and a three-year-old stereo.

The law protects consumers and this means that whenever you sell anything, you must be careful. You may not think about it, but whenever you have a garage sale or place an ad in the paper, you are governed by this law. Unless you are willing to stand by your word, be careful when you say something is "in excellent condition" or "good-as-new."

*Advice: If you are selling something, make sure the buyer knows you are just giving your opinion unless you are willing to stand by your word.* As the seller in the next letter discovers, you may be in trouble—even if you are acting innocently and in good faith.

## Is there a law regarding construction defects?
## "Yes, and it preempts the Deceptive Trade Practices Act."

*Dear Mr. Alderman:*
*I am a small independent contractor. I recently heard that the legis-lature passed a law that protects us when we are sued under the Deceptive Trade Practices Act. Is there such a law, and if there is, what does it say?*

You are right. There is a law that offers contractors additional protection when they are sued based on construction defects. This law is important to both consumers and contractors because the consumer who does not comply with the provisions of this law will collect substantially less in damages.

The law applies to any action to collect money from a contractor based on a construction defect, unless it is a personal injury action. Under the law, you must give notice to the contractor at least 60 days before filing suit, specifying in reasonable detail the defects that are the subject of the complaint. For 21 days after receiving this notice, the contractor has the right to inspect the defective property. Within 31 days after receiving notice, the contractor may make a written offer of settlement to the consumer. The offer may include an agreement to repair or have repaired the defects. The repairs must be made within 45 days, if the offer is accepted.

The most important aspect of this law arises when the consumer fails to accept the contractor's offer of settlement. If the consumer unreasonably rejects the settlement offer, he may not recover an amount in excess of the reasonable costs of the repairs and may only recover attorney's fees incurred up to the time the offer was rejected. In other words, before filing a claim under the Deceptive Trade Practices Act or any other law, you must give a contractor an opportunity to repair the defects, and if he does or offers to do so, you proceed with a lawsuit at your peril.

Here is a quick example of how the law works: Suppose that Tom hires a builder to repair his garage. After the work is completed and paid for, Tom discovers that the siding was not of the quality represented by the contractor. Tom wants to file suit under the Deceptive Trade Practices

Act for misrepresentation. Tom must first give the contractor 60 days notice of his complaint. He must then allow the contractor to come and look at the problem. If the contractor subsequently writes to Tom that he will change the siding at no cost, Tom must accept the offer, or else, if he sues, his damages will be limited to what it will cost to make the change. He also will not recover his attorney's fees for the lawsuit.

The construction industry must have had a good lobby during the 1989 session of the legislature to get this law passed. But the law really is not unfair. It simply says that before you sue for a construction defect, you must give the person a chance to make good on his promise.

### What if I didn't know it wasn't true? "Tough luck!"

*Dear Mr. Alderman:*
*I am a geologist. I have never been in the business of selling boats, and I have never sold one before. About one month ago, I decided to sell my small outboard motorboat. I took it to my mechanic, who said that he would put the engine in excellent shape. I paid him $500, and he told me it was "good as new." I put the boat, with the engine, in my front yard with a "for sale" sign. Someone I didn't know stopped and asked me about it. I told him the motor was in "excellent condition," "perfect condition," and "just like new." As far as I knew, these statements were true. What I didn't know was that my mechanic did not do the work. The buyer has now written me a letter telling me that he wants $450 (the cost of having the engine repaired). He says, unless I pay, he is going to sue me under the Deceptive Trade Practices Act and will recover three times the $450. What should I do? Does this law apply to me?*

As stated in response to the prior letter, the law applies to anyone who sells goods or services. This includes you—even though you are not in business. The Texas Deceptive Trade Practices Act is very broad. It protects consumers regardless of who deceives them.

The law is clear in that you do not have to have "intended" to deceive or trick someone. Your honesty or good faith does not matter. The law simply states that it is unlawful to misrepresent the nature of goods. You stated that the boat engine was in excellent condition, and it wasn't. That violates the act and, if proven, would entitle the buyer to three times his damages, plus his attorney's fees.

The best advice I can give you is to try to settle this with the buyer. Then contact the mechanic and tell him that you expect a reimbursement. If he refuses, you have a claim against him under the Deceptive Trade Practices Act. Next time, be careful.

*Remember: Whenever you sell anything, you are responsible for whatever you say. If you are not sure, don't say it, or make it clear that it is just your opinion.*

### What can I do about a "free" prize that wasn't really free? "The Deceptive Trade Practices Act may help."

*Dear Mr. Alderman:*
*I recently won a contest from a radio station. The "prize" was jewelry stated to be worth $10,800. I had the jewelry appraised, which came out to $5,400. A second appraisal said $2,700 was more like it. The station sent a Form 1099 to the IRS for $10,800 and my taxes on this free "prize" came to more than it was actually worth. Are there any laws prohibiting such false advertising by a radio station?*

First, as you now have found out, whenever you win a prize you must pay income taxes on the value of the prize. The question is, then, what is the value? I should point out that the value indicated in the Form 1099 is not necessarily the value you have to use for taxes. The IRS requires that you pay taxes on the fair market value. This is generally what a willing buyer would pay willing seller.

In your case, your estimates are as good an indication of this amount as is the 1099. You may want to protest the 1099 from the station and insist that they reissue one with a corrected amount. Additionally, if you sell the item you won, the IRS will usually use that amount as the value upon which you are required to pay taxes.

The question you ask, however, is a very good one. Are there laws regulating false advertising of contests? The simple answer is yes. False, misleading, or deceptive advertising is unlawful under the Texas Deceptive Trade Practices Act. The Attorney General enforces this law and could bring an action against any radio station that advertised falsely. The real issue under this law would be whether you as an individual would be entitled to damages.

To recover under this law, you must be a "consumer." This basically means you must be looking to "purchase" something. The free "prize" would not qualify unless you were required to do something to win. For example, if you had to purchase a product, count songs, send in a entry, or allow them to use you for publicity purposes, then, in my opinion, the prize had strings attached and was not "free." On the other hand, if you just called in and were given the prize, you probably do not have an individual claim under this law.

### The seller didn't say anything; am I out of luck?
### "There is a duty to speak."

*Dear Mr. Alderman:*
*I must have bought a "junker." It is a 1986 Oldsmobile, and I paid over $1,000 for it. As soon as I got it home, I found out the transmission was so bad that the car would not run for more than a few miles. I took it to the repair shop and they said it would cost nearly $800 to fix. They couldn't imagine how the seller wouldn't have known it. When I went back to the used car dealer, he admitted he knew the car needed a new transmission, but he said: "You didn't ask about the transmission and I didn't tell you about it. . . . What you saw is what you bought." Is this true? The car isn't worth more than a few hundred dollars in this condition. It seems to me the law should require someone to tell you when there is something wrong.*

The law is just what you assume it should be. Under the Texas Deceptive Trade Practices Act it is unlawful for a person to fail to disclose known defects if "such failure to disclose such information was intended to induce the consumer into a transaction which the consumer would not have entered into had the information been disclosed" (see Item 23, page 90).

In your case, if you can show that the dealer didn't disclose the information because he knew that you wouldn't pay the same price if you knew the car didn't work, the dealer would be violating the law. It doesn't matter that you didn't ask any questions. Your failure to inquire is not a defense to this law.

If the seller has violated the Deceptive Trade Practices Act, you are entitled to three times your damages. In your case your damages would be how much it will cost you to get the car into the condition it should have been in when you bought it: $800. As discussed in the letter on page 104, you will also be entitled to any court costs or attorney's fees that you incur.

The best advice I can give you is to contact the dealer, certified mail, return-receipt-requested, and tell him that you want your car fixed or money damages. Let him know that you know your rights under the Deceptive Trade Practices Act, and that, unless you can settle things, you will pursue your legal rights.

### The contract said "as is." Am I out of luck?
### "Not under the Deceptive Trade Practices Act."

*Dear Mr. Alderman:*
*I recently bought a used car. It was advertised in the paper as being in "excellent condition." When I looked at the car, the owner (he was not a dealer) told me that the car ran well and was in great shape mechanically. I bought it, and before I got it home it broke down. The mechanic says that the car is a piece of junk and is in terrible mechanical condition. When I asked for my money back, the seller told me to read the contract we had. I did and it says that the car is sold "as is." Am I out of luck? I guess it was my own fault for not reading the contract.*

Good news! The Deceptive Trade Practices Act may not be waived, even in a written contract. If a seller makes a statement of fact about a product and it is false, the seller is liable under the Deceptive Trade Practices Act, even though the written contract said otherwise. Saying that something is sold "as is" does have the legal effect of eliminating many warranties, but it does not change the Deceptive Trade Practices Act.

I suggest you talk to the seller and let him know that you know the law. As you probably already know, the Deceptive Trade Practices Act applies to any seller, even one not in business, and you could be entitled to three times your damages if you sue. I also should point out that the Texas Supreme Court has said that the good faith, intent, or knowledge of the seller who made the statement is irrelevant. If a misrepresentation is made, the Deceptive Trade Practices Act has usually been violated. The ad said "excellent condition" and it was not. Case closed.

### What can I do about something I paid for but never received?
### "That is unconscionable, and unlawful."

*Dear Mr. Alderman:*

*I made arrangements with an auto repair shop to rebuild my car's motor. I made payments until I had paid $750 in advance. The deal was that after I paid the $750, the mechanic would do the work. So far he has done nothing. I have tried numerous times to get them to make the repairs or give me my money back, and they won't. What are my rights?*

Fortunately for you, the Texas Deceptive Trade Practices Act applies to this situation. One of the things this law specifically deals with is people who take your money and give you nothing in return. Under the DTPA it is "unconscionable," and unlawful, to charge a price grossly in excess of value received. In other words, Texas law guarantees that you basically get what you paid for. One of the best examples of charging a grossly excessive price would be taking a deposit and not doing the work. I suggest you read the letter on page 104 about how to use this law, and let the mechanic know you know about the Deceptive Trade Practices Act.

### The real estate agent didn't tell me the former owner of the house died of AIDS. Doesn't this have to be disclosed? "Not under the law."

*Dear Mr. Alderman:*

*I just bought a new house. Right after I moved in I found out that the former owner of the house had died of AIDS, in the house. I don't want to sound like a crazy person but I am afraid of getting the disease. I probably would not have bought the house if I had known about this. I thought that the Texas Deceptive Trade Practices Act required that sellers disclose things like this. Do I have any legal rights?*

First, from everything I have heard or read there is no possibility of you contracting AIDS from living in a house where someone with the disease died. Hopefully, you will be able to enjoy the house and not worry about its prior occupants.

As far as your legal rights, you probably have none in this situation. You are right that the Deceptive Trade Practices Act, as well as the new real estate disclosure law discussed on page 98, requires a seller to disclose material facts to you if he knows these facts would matter. Under the law, a seller would probably have an obligation to tell you about the prior occupant's death. But the legislature recently passed a law that preempts the DTPA and allows people to remain silent with respect to AIDS. This law is consistent with federal laws that prohibit discrimination against persons with AIDS. The bottom line is that under present law there probably is no liability for the failure to disclose information regarding AIDS or related complexes to a prospective home buyer.

### No one told me the appliances didn't work. Do I have any rights? "Yes! There is a new disclosure law."

*Dear Mr. Alderman:*
*I recently bought a new house, actually a new used house. Everything looked to be in really good condition. The seller never told me that everything worked, but I assumed it did. Shortly after we moved in, we discovered that there were serious problems with the air conditioning unit. We didn't think to ask about this because it was winter when we bought the house. Are we just out of luck?*

Luckily for you, you bought your house after January 1st, 1994. Even though you may have rights under the Deceptive Trade Practices Act before this date, after it you are entitled to a full disclosure by the seller. Under the new law, a seller of residential real estate must give you written notice that contains certain required information. Although the notice does not have to be in any specific form, what follows is a copy of the form suggested by the legislature. If you did not receive such disclosures, you have the right to terminate the contract. You also may have a claim under the Deceptive Trade Practices Act. As a practical matter, however, my guess is that once the seller finds out about this he will promptly negotiate a fair settlement with you.

*(text continued on page 103)*

Example of the type of real estate disclosure statement now required by law.

SELLER'S DISCLOSURE NOTICE

CONCERNING THE PROPERTY AT _____

(Street Address and City)

THIS NOTICE IS A DISCLOSURE OF SELLER'S KNOWL-
EDGE OF THE CONDITION OF THE PROPERTY AS OF
THE DATE SIGNED BY SELLER AND IS NOT A SUBSTI-
TUTE FOR ANY INSPECTIONS OR WARRANTIES THE
PURCHASER MAY WISH TO OBTAIN. IT IS NOT A WAR-
RANTY OF ANY KIND BY SELLER OR SELLER'S
AGENTS.

Seller ___ is ___ is not occupying the property.

If unoccupied, how long since Seller has occupied the Property?___

_____

1. The Property has the items checked below:

Write Yes (Y), No (N), or Unknown (U).

| | | |
|---|---|---|
| ___ Range | ___ Oven | ___ Microwave |
| ___ Dishwasher | ___ Trash Compactor | ___ Disposal |
| ___ Washer/Dryer Hookups | ___ Window Screens | ___ Rain Gutters |
| ___ Security System | ___ Fire Detection Equipment | ___ Intercom System |
| ___ TV Antenna | ___ Cable TV Wiring | ___ Satellite Dish |
| ___ Ceiling Fan(s) | ___ Attic Fan(s) | ___ Exhaust Fan(s) |
| ___ Central A/C | ___ Central Heating | ___ Wall/Window Air Conditioning |
| ___ Plumbing System | ___ Septic System | ___ Public Sewer System |
| ___ Patio/Decking | ___ Outdoor Grill | ___ Fences |
| ___ Pool | ___ Sauna | ___ Spa |
| ___ Hot Tub | ___ Pool Equipment | ___ Pool Heater |

___ Automatic Lawn
   Sprinkler System
___ Fireplace(s) &        ___ Fireplace(s) &
   Chimney                   Chimney (Mock)
   (Woodburning)
___ Gas Lines             ___ Gas Fixtures
   (Nat./LP)

Garage:
___ Attached          ___ Not Attached       ___ Carport

Garage Door Opener(s):
___ Electronic        ___ Control(s)

Water Heater:
___ Gas               ___ Electric

Water Supply:
___ City              ___ Well               ___ MUD
___ Co-Op

Roof Type:_____

Age: ____(approx.)

2. Are you (Seller) aware of any of the above items that are not in working condition, that have known defects, or that are in need of repair?

   ___ Yes ___No ___Unknown

   If yes, then describe. (Attach additional sheets if necessary):

   _____
   _____
   _____

3. Are you (Seller) aware of any known defects/malfunctions in any of the following? Write Yes (Y) if you are, write No (N) if you are not aware.
   ___ Interior Walls    ___ Ceilings      ___ Floors
   ___ Exterior Walls    ___ Doors         ___ Windows
   ___ Roof              ___ Foundation/   ___ Basement
                            Slab(s)

___ Walls/Fences       ___ Driveways       ___ Sidewalks
___ Plumbing/          ___ Electrical      ___ Lighting
    Sewers/Septics       Systems          Fixtures

Other Structural Components (Describe):

_____

_____

_____

If the answer to any of the above is yes, explain. (Attach additional sheets if necessary):

_____

_____

_____

4. Are you (Seller) aware of any of the following conditions?
___ Active Termites        ___ Previous Structural or Roof Repair
    (includes wood-destroying insects)
___ Termite or Wood Rot Damage
___ Hazardous or Toxic Waste
Needing Repair:
___ Asbestos Components
___ Previous Termite Damage
___ Urea Formaldehyde Insulation
___ Previous Termite Treatment
___ Radon Gas             ___ Lead Based Paint    ___ Previous
                                                Flooding
___ Aluminum Wiring ___ Improper Drainage   ___ Previous Fires
___ Water Penetration ___ Located in 100-Year
                        Floodplain
___ Unplatted Easements
___ Present Flood Insurance Coverage
___ Landfill, Settling, Soil
___ Subsurface Structure or Pits
___ Movement, Fault Lines

If the answer to any of the above is yes, explain. (Attach additional sheets if necessary):

_____

_____

5. Are you (Seller) aware of any item, equipment, or system in or on the property that is in need of repair? _____ Yes (if you are aware) _____ No (if you are not aware). If yes, explain (attach additional sheets if necessary):

_____

6. Are you (Seller) aware of any of the following?
Write Yes (Y) if you are aware, write No (N) if you are not aware.
____ Room additions, structural modifications, or other alterations or repairs made without necessary permits or not in compliance with building codes in effect at that time.
____ Homeowners' Association or maintenance fees or assessments.
____ Any "common area" (facilities such as pools, tennis courts, walkways, or other areas) co-owned in undivided interest with others.
____ Any notices of violations of deed restrictions or governmental ordinances affecting the condition or use of the Property.
____ Any lawsuits directly or indirectly affecting the Property.
____ Any condition on the Property which materially affects the physical health or safety of an individual.

If the answer to any of the above is yes, explain. (Attach additional sheets if necessary):

_____
_____
_____
_____


_____          _____
Date                                                     Signature of Seller


The undersigned purchaser hereby acknowledges receipt of the foregoing notice.


_____          _____
Date                                                     Signature of Purchaser

*(text continued from page 98)*

## What are "treble" damages?
## "Good news for you."

*Dear Mr. Alderman:*
*I have heard you speak about the Deceptive Trade Practices Act,*
*and the fact that it allows you to recover "treble" damages. Just*
*what does this mean?*

The Deceptive Trade Practices Act is designed to do two things: first, to compensate consumers for their losses and, second, to deter people from engaging in false or deceptive practices. To deter wrongdoers, the law enables you to collect what may be viewed as punitive damages, damages designed to "punish" the wrongdoer, not just to compensate you for your loss.

If a claim is for less than $1,000, a successful consumer automatically receives three times his damages, plus attorney's fees. For example, suppose you purchase a new television and it doesn't work. The store manager refuses to repair it, even though there was a warranty. You can sue the merchant for breach of warranty, which is always a violation of the Deceptive Trade Practices Act. Your damages, in this case, would be the amount it cost you to have the television repaired.

Let's say another dealer fixed it for $150; if you could not recover the $150 from the dealer and had to sue, you would be entitled to recover three times that amount, or $450. This is what is commonly referred to as "treble" damages. You could recover, also, your court costs and attorney's fees.

If the amount is over $1,000, you recover three times the first $1,000, but the amount over $1,000 is trebled only if the court finds the act was committed "knowingly." In my example, the merchant obviously knew that he was refusing to repair the set and, therefore, all damages, even in excess of $1,000, could be multiplied by three. But consider the following example.

Suppose the dealer told you a car was a 1956 Chevy and sold you the car for $6,500—a fair price for a 1956 model. It turns out, however, the previous owner had changed some parts and the car was really a 1957, worth only $5,000. The dealer misrepresented the nature of the car, so he has violated the Deceptive Trade Practices Act. Your damages would be $1,500, the difference in value between the two models. In this case, however, the court would only triple the first $1,000, due to the fact that the dealer did not knowingly violate the law. Your recovery would be $3,000 (the first $1,000 times 3), plus $500 (the rest of your damages), for a total of $3,500. You would also recover your attorney's fees and court costs.

The possibility of treble damages is what lends teeth to the Deceptive Trade Practices Act. *Once a person knows he may have to pay a large sum if he loses in court, he is more likely to treat you fairly and try to settle.* Make sure the seller is aware that you know the law and how much his damages may be. My guess is that you will quickly be able to work out an agreeable settlement.

### How do I use the Deceptive Trade Practices Act
### "It's simple."

*Dear Mr. Alderman:*
*I have heard about the consumer protection law in Texas called the Deceptive Trade Practices Act. From what I have been told, this could be just the law to help me with a problem I'm having with my mechanic. I was just wondering—is there anything special I have to do to utilize this law? Can I go to small claims court? I only want the $75 he took from me.*

The Deceptive Trade Practices Act allows a consumer to recover three times his or her damages plus court costs and attorney's fees, if any. But if you are going to use this law there are a few steps you *must* follow.

*First,* remember you cannot go to small claims court if the amount of money you are asking for is over $5,000, *and this may include the tripled amount.* For example, you say you have been damaged in the amount of $75. Under this law you would ask for three times that, or $225, which is well within the $2,500 limit. But what if your damages were $3,000? Because three times this is $9,000, you may not be able to go to small claims court. You would need an attorney to sue for you in county court or district court. Of course, you could still sue for the $3,000 in small claims court; you either must not state that the person acted "knowingly" or not sue under the Deceptive Trade Practices Act.

*Next,* once you decide to use this law, you must give written notice of your problem at least 60 days before you file your claim in court. The notice must give the specific nature of the claim in reasonable detail and the amount of actual damages, including attorney's fees if any. The following letter could be used as a model:

---

Mr. C. Consumer<br>
435 Central Dr.<br>
Consumer, TX 77597

Dear Mr. Merchant:

On Wednesday, June 16, I brought my car into your shop to be repaired. I told you to tune it up and you stated that it would cost $49.95. This is the same amount advertised in the paper the day before. When I picked up my car you charged me $124.95. You told me that the $49.95 was for imports only. This was not stated in the ad or told to me before.

I feel your conduct in stating one price and charging another is a false and deceptive practice under the Texas Deceptive Trade Practices Act. I have been damaged in the amount of $75.

Under the law I must give you 60 days' notice of my complaint prior to filing a claim. Unless I receive a satisfactory settlement from you within that period I intend to pursue my claim in court. I should point out that if I am successful I will be entitled to three times my damages.

Thank you for your expected cooperation.

Sincerely yours,<br>
C. Consumer

---

*During the 60 days, the person you notified has the right to inspect any goods that are part of your complaint. The purpose of the notice requirement is to give the other party a chance to settle the case without costly litigation.* Under the law, if the other side offers a settlement and you refuse it, and if then the court awards substantially the same amount, you are not entitled to three times your damages. *If you are offered a settlement substantially the same as what you asked for, you should accept.*

If you do not give the proper notice, you may not be entitled to collect at all, so make sure to send your notice certified mail, return-receipt-requested, so you have proof it was sent. And be sure to include a description of what it is that you think the person has done that violates the law, and exactly how much your damages are.

One final comment: Should you see an attorney? The simple answer is: It is up to you. If the amount is less than $5,000, small claims court is simple to use, and quick. But an attorney may increase your potential for recovery and may know of damages you are entitled to that you overlooked. But litigation with an attorney takes a long time and costs money. You must balance all these factors and make the decision yourself. You may want to talk with an attorney before going to small claims court, just to get an idea of how he or she could help.

# Immigration*

$F$EW areas of law have sparked as much public interest and controversy as immigration law. Immigration law determines who has the right to live and work in the United States. As you might imagine, this area of law is of great concern to many people.

The most common questions that arise concerning immigration law involve the rights of "undocumented aliens" to live and work in the United States, legally. Recent changes in the law, brought about by the Immigration Reform and Control Act of 1986 (the IRCA) allow more people to legally remain in this country, but they also have caused much concern. The following questions and answers may help resolve some of this uncertainty.

### What should I do to see if I can legally stay in the U.S.?
### "First contact an INS-designated counseling center."

*Dear Mr. Alderman:*
*I have come to Texas illegally from Honduras and now want to stay here. However, I have been told that if I am discovered I will be deported. I have been here almost 10 years and have a good job and my wife is here legally. I am thinking of quitting my job because I am afraid of being caught. Is there anything I can do to stay here legally? Is there any organization that can help me?*

There are several laws that may provide you with an opportunity to remain in the U.S. For example, depending on how your wife is here legally you may be entitled to remain here. The first thing you should do is see an immigration counselor at one of the INS-designated counseling centers in Texas. Here is a list of some of the centers:

---

* I must give special thanks to Professor Michael Olivas of the University of Houston Law Center
  for assisting me with the preparation of this chapter.

107

## Austin
- Cristo Vive for Immigrants, 7524 N. Lamar, Suite 106-10.
- Austin Travis County Refugee Service, 111 Montopolis Drive.
- SER—JOBS For Progress, 55 North I-H 35, Suite 102.
- Austin Travis County Refugee Service, 1607 W. 6th Street.
- The Episcopal Church of the Good Shepherd, 2206 Exposition Blvd.
- Holy Trinity Episcopal Church, 1705 Mariposa Drive.

## Beaumont
- Catholic Diocese of Beaumont, 2625 S. 4th St.
- St. Stephen's Episcopal Church, 4090 Delaware.

## Beeville
- St. Philip's Episcopal Church, 311 E. Corpus Christi.

## Brownsville
- St. Paul's Episcopal Church, 1626 E. Taft Street.

## Bryan
- St. Andrew's Episcopal Church, 217 W. 26th, Box 405.
- Diocesan Migrant and Refugee Services, 1200 North Mesa.
- United States Catholic Conference, 1200 North Mesa, Suite 201.
- LICEO Sylvan Center, 3021 Fritas.

## Burnet
- Catholic Social Services, 500 Buchanan, Suite B.

## Corpus Christi
- St. Martin's Episcopal Church, 1641 G. Cliff.
- Catholic Social Services, 1650 S. Brownlee Blvd.
- SER—JOBS For Progress, 1201 South Point Avenue.
- St. Thomas Episcopal Church, 4100 Up River Road.

## Crystal City
- Community Agency for Self Help, 722 E. Crockett Street.

## Dallas
- Northcutt Immigration Assistance Center Mary King. Memorial UMC.
- SER—JOBS For Progress, 2514 Harry Hines Blvd.
- SER—JOBS For Progress, 1355 River Bend Dr. Diocese of Dallas, 3845 Oaklawn Ave.
- Northcutt Immigration Assistance, 5111 Capitol.

## Eagle Pass
- Redeemer Episcopal Church, 648 Madison Street.
- Jim Haynes, 470 N. Monroe Street.

## Fort Pierce
- Agricultural and Labor Program, Inc., 1814 N. 13th St.

## Fort Worth
- Catholic Charities, 1404 Hemphill St.

- World Relief, 4567 James Ave., Suite B.
- San Juan Episcopal Church, 3725 S. Adams.

**Galveston**
- SER—JOBS For Progress, 3901 Avenue M½.

**Houston**
- Refugee Service Alliance, 2808 Caroline St.
- SER—JOBS For Progress, 2150 West 18th Street, Suite 300.
- Lutheran Social Services of Texas, 3131 W. Alabama, Suite 124.
- YMCA International Service, 2903 W. Dallas St.
- Episcopal Church of the Redeemer, 4411 Dallas Ave.

**Laredo**
- Christ Episcopal Church, 2320 Lane Street

**Longview**
- Trinity Episcopal Church, 906 Padon St.

**Lubbock**
- Catholic Family Service, 123 North Ave. N.

**Midland**
- Diocese of San Angelo, 1203 N. Big Spring.

**Nacogdoches**
- Christ Episcopal Church, 502 E. Starr St.

**Pasadena**
- St. Peter's Episcopal Church, 705 Williams.

**Pharr**
- Trinity Episcopal Church, 210 W. Caffery Street.

**San Antonio**
- San Antonio Literacy Council, 1101 W. Woodlawn.
- SER—JOBS For Progress, 525 Cupples Road.
- Santa Fe Episcopal Church, 1108 Brunswick.
- Diocesan Migrant and Refugee Services, 1200 North Mesa.
- Holy Cross Episcopal Church, 379 E. Petaluma.

**Tyler**
- Christ Episcopal Church, 118 S. Bois D'Arc St.

**Victoria**
- Diocese of Victoria in Texas, 1505 E. Mesquite Lane.

**Waco**
- St. Paul's Episcopal Church, 515 Columbus Avenue.

**Weslaco**
- Grace Episcopal Church, 701 S. Missouri.
- Catholic Family Service, 1422 S. Tyler, Suite 200.

*One final note:* Your local Bar Association may have some volunteer agencies or lawyers they can recommend. You may also want to contact the Mexican American Legal Defense and Education fund in San Antonio (512) 224-5476. They do not counsel individual clients, but they do initiate suits for groups of Hispanics who are discriminated against, and can recommend Spanish-speaking lawyers.

## Who can get amnesty?
## "The law has expired."

*Dear Mr. Alderman:*
*I have heard and read a lot about the new amnesty law but I am afraid to contact anyone official until I know if I am covered. It would be a big help if you could just briefly explain who is eligible for amnesty and what could happen to me if I went to apply and wasn't eligible. Can I be deported? Do I have to give my address?*

Under the Immigration Reform and Control Act of 1986, commonly just referred to as the IRCA, the following persons were eligible for amnesty:

A. *In general.* The alien must establish that he or she entered the United States before January 1, 1982, and that he or she has resided continuously in the United States in an unlawful status since such date and through the date the application is filed.

B. *Nonimmigrants.* In the case of an alien who entered the United States as a nonimmigrant before January 1, 1982, the alien must establish that the alien's period of authorized stay as a nonimmigrant expired before such date through the passage of time or the alien's unlawful status was known to the Government as of such date.

C. *Exchange visitors.* If the alien was at any time a nonimmigrant exchange alien, he or she must establish that he or she was not subject to the two-year foreign residence requirement, or has fulfilled that requirement or received a waiver.

I say "were" because the law expired on May 5, 1988. The amnesty law was a one-shot chance for people to legally stay in this country. Now that it has expired you must qualify under another law if you want to remain here legally. To find out if there is a provision in the law that may help you, I suggest you contact one of the agencies listed on pages 108–109.

### What does someone from another country need to visit this country?
### "A visa."

*Dear Mr. Alderman:*
*I have a friend in another country that wants to come and visit me*
*for awhile. I have heard all of the complaints about "illegal aliens,"*
*and I want to know what she has to do to make sure she complies*
*with the law while she lives with me.*

Basically, to enter the United States from another country you must
have the permission of the United States. This permission is called a
"visa." Your friend can obtain a visa from the American consul. Because
she is only coming to temporarily visit you, she can obtain a nonimmi-
gration visa. These are issued to people who plan on staying in the United States temporarily. For example, a nonimmigrant visa can be used by
a businessperson who is coming only to work for his company, a student
who will be attending school, or a tourist, such as your friend.

I should point out that a tourist visa authorizes your friend to stay here,
but not to work here. She also must return after the visa expires unless
she has it extended, or changes her status to an immigrant visa.

### What is a green card?
### "The right to stay in the United States."

*Dear Mr. Alderman:*
*I am an American citizen and have never really paid much attention*
*to immigration laws. Now that I own a small business, I have been*
*told that I shouldn't hire any aliens unless they have a green card.*
*Just what is a green card?*

As I said in the letter right before this one, someone from another
country can be in this country legally only if he or she has permission.
The law prohibits you from hiring an alien who is not properly documented. For example, a worker with a worker's visa would be properly
documented and could be hired to work for you. A visa is the document
given to aliens who are here temporarily.

If an alien wants to reside in this country permanently, and wants the
right to come in and go out of the United States, he or she must obtain an
Alien Registration Receipt Card. Although this card is no longer green,
its common name is still a "green card." Not everyone, however, can get

a green card. To receive one, you basically must show that you have family here, you are a worker entitled to special treatment, or you are a businessperson making a large investment in this country.

The most common way of obtaining a green card is by having a family relationship with someone in this country. For example, if you are a spouse, child, parent, brother, or sister, or are engaged to an American citizen, you can become a permanent resident. To do this, the person you have the relationship with must file an application with the INS or the American Embassy of the country where the alien lives. You also can obtain a green card if you are the spouse or child of a person with a green card. In this case, the relative who is a permanent resident of the United States must file the application. Although it is less common, permanent resident status can also be obtained if you have a job that this country considers a priority. For example, scientists, professors, or high level business executives may be eligible to remain in this country as permanent residents.

Finally, the Immigration Act of 1994 allows 55,000 immigrants from certain countries to come to the United States as permanent residents without the need to meet the above requirements. The countries are those that have sent the fewest immigrant to this country in the past. The INS can give you the list of countries whose citizens are considered "diversity immigrants."

### What is a "notary"?
### "Not a lawyer or a notario"

*Dear Mr. Alderman:*
*I am from Mexico and I wanted legal advice in Dallas, where I live. I went to a notary public where they said for $500 they would help me with my problem. What is a notary public? Is it a "notario" (lawyer)?*

In Mexico and other Spanish speaking countries, a "notario" performs many of the same functions as an attorney. In the United States, a notary public is *not* an attorney, and cannot hold himself out as a lawyer to represent you in court or in other legal proceedings. Basically, all a notary public does is attest to signatures or certify that you signed a document, and perform some other clerking services. Nearly anyone can become a notary public just by paying a small fee.

If you need legal services, see an attorney ("abogado" or "licenciado"). If you think the notary public misrepresented himself or engaged in unauthorized legal work, you should report him to the district attorney's office, the attorney general, or the State Bar of Texas (1-800-932-1900). The unauthorized practice of law is a crime.

And by the way, notaries usually charge very little for their services. Beware of anyone charging a high fee for performing his or her duties as a notary public.

### I am afraid to go home. What can I do?
### "You may be entitled to asylum."

*Dear Mr. Alderman:*
*I am from El Salvador and fled to the U.S. because my brother was killed by government soldiers and I heard they were looking for me, too. Is there any way I can stay in the United States, at least until things get better in my country and it is safe for me to return?*

You should seek assistance from an immigration attorney or the counseling agencies listed on pages 108–109. If you have reason to believe you may be harmed, you may be eligible for *asylum* "because of persecution on account of race, religion, nationality, membership in a particular social group, or political opinion." These are highly technical terms, but an attorney or qualified immigration counselor could help you apply for asylum if you qualify. You are entitled to a series of legal rights and hearings, and may even be eligible to work in the U.S. Even more than other persons, however, you should be careful not to commit a crime or break a law, because any immigration hearings will include a record of your time and behavior while in the U.S.

### I am a U.S. citizen, but I still am asked for ID.
### Is this legal?
### "Everyone must show they are eligible to work."

*Dear Mr. Alderman:*
*I am a citizen, but I notice that my union won't hire anybody without ID or a "green card." Is this legal? I am a third-generation American and I resent having to prove that I am "legal."*

Employers must screen all new employees (those hired since November 6, 1986) to determine if they are eligible to work. However, they must ask the same questions and require the same papers of *everyone,* not just people who may "look Mexican," or who speak with an accent. There are no sanctions for employers who hired undocumented employees before November 6, 1986, but there may be penalties for people hired after that date. *All* employees must be treated equally in the hiring process.

## Does my child have to have a social security number to stay in school?
## "No!"

*Dear Mr. Alderman:*
*My daughter brought home a letter from school that said all school children must have social security numbers and that we should fill out forms to get an SS number. I'm afraid not to get one, or they might not let my daughter stay in school. What can I do?*

*No child* has to have a Social Security Number to enroll in school. Even undocumented children can attend public schools if their parents reside in the school district. Last year's tax law makes changes in who may be eligible for a tax deduction, but you are not required to take any action that exposes you or your children to possible deportation. As with any such case involving immigration, you should consult an attorney or reputable immigration counseling center. (See pages 108–109.)

## I am a small employer; must I comply with the immigration law?
## "Probably yes."

*Dear Mr. Alderman:*
*I have a small business, delivering documents for local firms. I employ about 5–10 people. The other day someone told me that I could get in trouble if I didn't comply with the immigration law. I*

*don't have anyone working for me who is not a permanent resident or U.S. citizen; do I still have to bother with this law?*

Yes. The law applies to nearly everyone who employs someone to perform work or labor or services in return for wages. Under the law you must complete what is called a Form I-9 for:

- *Persons hired after May 31, 1987.* For these employees, you must complete a Form I-9 within three business days of the date of the hire. (If you employ the person for less than three days, you must complete the Form I-9 before the end of the employee's first working day.)
- *Persons hired between November 7, 1986 and May 31, 1987.* For these employees, you must have completed Form I-9 before September 1, 1987.

*Note:* If you employ people for domestic work in your private home on a regular (such as weekly) basis, these requirements also apply to you.

You *do not* need to complete Form I-9 for:

- Persons hired before November 7, 1986.
- Persons hired after November 6, 1986, who left your employment before June 1, 1987.
- Persons you employ for domestic work in a private home on an intermittent or sporadic basis.
- Persons who provide labor to you who are employed by a contractor providing contract services (e.g., employee leasing).
- Persons who are independent contractors.

Form I-9 is designed to verify that people are eligible to work in the United States. The form is easy to complete and there is a free book available to help you. To get the book, write or contact the U.S. Immigration Service and ask for the *Handbook for Employers: Instructions for Completing Form I-9.*

*Note:* You can be fined if you do not comply with this law, and don't try to get around it by not hiring anyone you think may be unauthorized to work here. Under the law it is also unlawful for a business with four or more employees to discriminate against any individual because of that person's national origin or citizenship status. In other words, ask for papers from everyone you hire, not just minority workers.

# CHAPTER TWELVE

# Landlord & Tenant Rights

**"L**ANDLORD-TENANT" law is centuries old and, for most of that time, it has been very one-sided. Landlord-tenant law historically has favored the landlord. But recently, there have been some changes, and while you may not have all the rights you would like, you are not without recourse.

Two laws in particular give you rights against the landlord when he doesn't keep up the apartment or when he doesn't return your security deposit.

*The most important part of any landlord-tenant relationship is the lease. Read yours carefully before you sign. If you don't like something in the lease, don't sign until the landlord agrees to remove it.*

### Do I need a lease?
### "No, but it can help."

*Dear Mr. Alderman:*
*I just moved to the city. I found an apartment that I liked and told the landlord I would take it. He said, "Fine, you can move in on the first." When I asked for a lease he told me not to worry, he never uses them. Now I am worried. Is it legal to rent an apartment without a lease? What if he just throws me out?*

A landlord-tenant relationship is created by an agreement called a lease. This agreement can be oral or written, and can be as informal or formal as the parties want to make it. *There is no requirement that you have a formal lease to rent an apartment.*

If you do not have a written lease, the law implies a lease for at least as long as the period between rent payments. For example, if you agree to pay rent once a month, the law says you have a month-to-month lease. This means that neither you nor the landlord may terminate the agreement without giving at least one month's notice to the other. If you were paying rent once a week, your agreement would be weekly, and one week's notice of termination would be required.

In your case, you can have an implied lease with your landlord; however, it is only a month-to-month agreement. This means you can only leave, or be evicted, after 30 days' notice. If you want a longer guarantee, you may want a written lease. You also may want to have a written lease so that all of the terms of your agreement are spelled out. This is a good way to avoid later problems that might arise concerning who is obligated to do what; for example, who pays for utilities or repairs.

As far as your question about the landlord just throwing you out, you should read the next letter.

### If I am late with my rent, can my landlord just throw me out? "No, you can be evicted only after a court hearing and only by a constable or sheriff."

*Dear Mr. Alderman:*
*I was recently laid off and I don't have enough money to pay my bills. I am already one month late in my rent. I just received a notice from my landlord to vacate. It says that if I am not out in three days he will have me evicted. I have a place to move but it won't be ready for a week. Does the landlord have the right to throw me out in the street in three days?*

No. Under the law a landlord cannot personally evict a tenant. You may only be evicted after: 1) the landlord commences a legal proceeding against you; 2) you have an opportunity to appear in court; 3) the judge orders you to leave; and 4) you do not leave. Even then the eviction must be done by a constable or sheriff pursuant to a court order.

If your landlord were to throw you out he would be responsible for any damages you suffered, and may even be liable for criminal and civil penalties. I suggest that you talk to your landlord and tell him that you are moving out, and will be out in a few days. It will take the landlord at least that long to have you evicted legally and he may prefer just to cooperate.

I should emphasize one point. Even though you are moving out you are still responsible for the rent that you owe, including rent for the period remaining on your lease after you move. Your landlord has the right to sue to try to collect this money.

## When can I move out?
## "Read your lease."

*Dear Mr. Alderman:*
*My company just transferred me to another city. When I gave my landlord a 30-day notice, he told me my lease still had six months left. I told him I was transferred, and there was no way I could stay. He told me that if he couldn't rent the apartment to someone else, I would have to pay the six months' rent. This does not seem fair. Don't I have the right to move if I am transferred?*

This may not be what you want to hear, but unless your lease says so, you do not have the right to move out if you are transferred and you may be responsible for rent for the remainder of the lease term. *A lease is a binding legal agreement and you are controlled by its terms. You may only terminate a lease early for reasons permitted by the lease.* For example, if your lease says you may terminate, by giving 30 days' notice, if you are transferred, you are all right. But if the lease is silent as to early termination, you may not terminate early just because you have been transferred. If you do terminate early you may be responsible for all the damages the landlord incurs, including the rent for the period that he cannot lease the apartment to someone else.

If you do not have a lease agreement, the law will imply one for the period of time between rent payments. For example, if you pay rent once a month, the law will create what is called a month-to-month tenancy. This type of arrangement can be terminated by either the tenant or the landlord, *for any reason,* by giving one month's notice. A lease protects you, by ensuring that the landlord does not terminate the lease or raise the rent, but it also protects the landlord by obligating you for the entire period of the lease. *If you think you may have to terminate your lease early, make sure that there is a clause permitting you to do so. Otherwise, you may end up owing rent on two apartments.*

## What if I don't get my security deposit back?
## "There's a law."

*Dear Mr. Alderman:*
*My apartment was a dump. The landlady never fixed it and as soon as my lease was up, I moved. Now, my landlady refuses to return my*

*security deposit. I have called her and written many times and she just won't respond. Don't Texas tenants have any rights?*

Your landlady may not wrongfully keep your security deposit. If she does, you may be entitled to three times your deposit, plus an additional $100 and any court costs or attorney's fees you may incur.

A law known as the **Texas Security Deposit Law,** which may not be waived or changed by your lease, requires a landlord to return a security deposit within 30 days after the tenant moves out or give the tenant written notice as to why the deposit is being kept.

It is important to remember that you are only entitled to have your deposit returned to you if you complied with your lease and left the apartment in good condition. For example: If you move before your lease is up, you may not be entitled to the return of the deposit. A landlord can also deduct the costs of cleaning the apartment if you left it damaged. *No damages may be deducted for ordinary wear-and-tear.*

If your landlady has not returned your deposit within 30 days, or written you why it was not returned, you should send her a certified letter, return-receipt-requested, to make certain she has your forwarding address. You should also tell her that should you not get your deposit back soon, you will take advantage of the security deposit law. You can use the following letter as a model.

---

Landlord Name
Street Address
City, State, Zip

Dear Landlord:

On (<u>fill in date</u>) I moved out of the house/apartment that I was renting from you. As our lease agreement provided, I gave proper notice and left the apartment in good condition. I was also current in my rent.

When I moved in, I paid a security deposit of (<u>amount</u>). You have not returned my deposit as the law requires. Under the law, a landlord must refund a security deposit or send written notice of the reasons it is being withheld within 30 days after the tenant vacates the property.

---

*(letter continued on next page)*

*(letter continued from previous page)*

> Unless I receive my security deposit from you within a reasonable time, I intend to go to small claims court. I should tell you that if I do go to court, I may be entitled to three times the amount of my deposit plus $100.
>
> Thank you for your expected cooperation in this matter. If you need to reach me, my present address is: (street address).
>
> Sincerely,
> (sign your name)

(Send this letter certified mail, return-receipt-requested, 30 days after you move out, if your security deposit has not been returned.)

If you still do not receive your deposit or written notice, consider small claims court. Under the law, a landlord who acts in bad faith in not returning your deposit may be liable for three times the deposit plus $100 in additional damages. *If the landlord does not return your money or give you a written explanation, the burden will be on the landlord to prove that he did not act in bad faith.* The burden is also on the landlord to prove that any deductions, such as money taken out for cleaning, were reasonable.

The Texas Security Deposit Law is one of the few landlord-tenant laws that really help the tenant. It is my experience that once the landlord *knows* that *you know* about this law, he quickly returns your deposit. Just sending the form letter should be enough to retrieve your money.

### What if my landlord won't fix my apartment?
### "Keep paying rent."

*Dear Mr. Alderman:*
*Nothing in my apartment works right. It seems every day something else is breaking, and it always takes the landlord weeks to fix it. Even though the problems are small, it is still an inconvenience. Last week, for example, I had to use a wrench to turn the stove on and off. Right now there are six things wrong, and it has been one week since I reported them. What I would like to do is just not pay my rent until everything is fixed. My landlord keeps saying he will fix it but never does. What do you recommend?*

The first thing I should point out is that, unless your lease says so, your landlord does not have a general obligation to repair the property. Recently, however, a law was passed that requires a landlord to repair conditions that materially affect physical health or safety. This law is discussed in the next letter, and it doesn't seem to apply to your problem. Small inconveniences, such as problems with a door or a drawer in the kitchen, or the knobs on an appliance, are not the responsibility of the landlord *unless* he has agreed to make these repairs.

So what should you do? First, read your lease. See if the landlord has undertaken to repair your apartment. If he has, you should contact him, in writing, and request that he make the necessary repairs. If he still refuses, you can make them yourself and recover the amount it costs from him in small claims court. You cannot, however, deduct the amount from your rent unless the landlord agrees.

Even if the lease does not say anything about repairs, your landlord may still be responsible if he has otherwise agreed to make repairs. From what you say, the landlord has repaired the apartment before and seems to understand that this is his obligation. Assuming that you can show that he has agreed to make repairs, then he would be responsible just as if it were in the lease.

The law generally does not impose an obligation on the landlord to repair your apartment, *and in most cases you must continue to pay rent regardless of whether your apartment needs repairs.* But there is an exception to this general rule. As the next letter shows, if the condition is serious enough, the law makes the landlord repair it, and lets you move or withhold from your rent if he doesn't.

### What can I do if the apartment is in such bad shape I can't live in it?
### "The warranty of habitability applies here."

*Dear Mr. Alderman:*
*I need help! The roof in my apartment leaks and the landlord won't fix it. The leak keeps getting worse, and now when it rains I have to go somewhere else to sleep. Is there any way I can force the landlord to fix this place? I don't want to move, because moving is so expensive.*

First of all, *do not stop paying rent.* Under the law, even if you have a claim against your landlord for not maintaining your apartment, you are not excused from paying rent until you take the necessary steps. *If you stop paying rent, your landlord could have you evicted.* Here is what you have to do to withhold rent or get damages.

In 1979, the Texas legislature passed a law requiring that a landlord make a reasonable effort to repair or remedy any condition which materially affects the health or safety of an ordinary tenant once the tenant gives the landlord notice of the problem. This law imposes an obligation on the landlord to make sure that your apartment is "habitable." If the landlord does not comply with this law you may be entitled to withhold rent and have the repairs made yourself; or, get a rent reduction and a penalty of one month's rent plus $500; or, you may have the right to terminate the lease and move out. Recent amendments to the law allow you to have the condition repaired yourself, and the amount deducted from your rent, if:

(a) The landlord has failed to remedy the backup or overflow of raw sewage inside the tenant's dwelling or the flooding from broken pipes or natural drainage inside the dwelling.

(b) The landlord has expressly or impliedly agreed in the lease to furnish potable water to the tenant's dwelling and the water service to the dwelling has totally ceased.

(c) The landlord has expressly or impliedly agreed in the lease to furnish heating or cooling equipment; the equipment is producing inadequate heat or cooled air; and the landlord has been notified in writing by the appropriate local housing, building, or health official or other official having jurisdiction, that the lack of heat or cooling materially affects the health or safety of an ordinary tenant.

(d) The landlord has been notified in writing by the appropriate local housing, building, or health official or other official having jurisdiction that the condition materially affects the health or safety of an ordinary tenant.

*Here is how the law works:* First, you must give your landlord written notice of the problems with your apartment. I recommend you send this notice via certified mail, return-receipt-requested. Explain the problem, and tell the landlord that it materially affects your health and safety. Next, under the law the landlord has a reasonable time to repair the problem. What is reasonable depends on the facts of the situation, but a leaking roof is serious and I would say that a few days is a reasonable time.

*If your apartment is not repaired within a reasonable time, you must give the landlord a second notice that unless the condition is repaired you will terminate the lease, repair the condition yourself, or bring a civ-*

*il action for damages.* If you terminate the lease, you will be entitled to a refund of any rent paid for the period after you move out. If you want to stay there, but want damages, you can sue by yourself in small claims court for up to $5,000 in damages, or you can have the repairs done yourself and withhold the cost from your rent.

In summary:

1. Texas law imposes an obligation on landlords to make a diligent effort to repair any condition that materially affects the physical health or safety of a reasonable tenant.
2. You must give the landlord notice of the condition and a reasonable time to repair it.
3. If it is not repaired you must give the landlord a second notice that if it is not repaired you will either terminate the lease, seek damages, or have the repairs made and the cost deducted from your rent.
4. If the landlord doesn't repair the condition you have the right to move out, have the condition repaired, sue and force a rent reduction, or recover damages of a month's rent plus $500. If you have to hire an attorney, the landlord must pay your attorney's fees if you win.

Here are some form letters you can use to show your landlord you are serious and that you know the law. Send the following letter after your landlord hasn't made the repairs. Send it certified mail, return-receipt-requested. Be sure to keep a copy.

---

Landlord
Landlord Street
City, Texas 77000

Dear Landlord:

On (<u>fill in date</u>) I discovered that [state nature of problem] my roof was leaking.

This condition materially affects the health and safety of an ordinary tenant. I have in no way caused or contributed to this condition.

Please repair this condition immediately. If you need more information or would like to arrange for a repair person to enter my

---

*(letter continued on next page)*

*(letter continued from previous page)*

> apartment, I can be reached during the day at (phone number) and in the evening at (phone).
>    Thank you for your expected cooperation in this matter.
>
> Sincerely yours,
> Your Name

If, after a reasonable period of time, repairs are not made, send the following letter. Send it certified mail, return-receipt-requested. Be sure to keep a copy.

> Landlord
> Landlord Street
> City, Texas 77000
> Dear Landlord:
>
>    On (fill in date) I wrote you concerning (state nature of problem) my leaky roof. I have attached a copy of that letter.
>    It has now been more than a reasonable time to make repairs and you have not fixed it. As I told you in my earlier letter, this condition materially affects my physical health and safety.
>    Unless the repairs are made to my apartment immediately, I intend either to terminate the lease, seek damages for your failure to repair, or have the condition repaired and withhold the cost from my rent. I should advise you that, under the law, I may be entitled to a refund of any rent already paid if I terminate, or a penalty of one month's rent plus $500, and court costs and attorney's fees if I seek damages.
>    I hope that it will not be necessary for me to take any further action. Thank you for your expected cooperation.
>
> Sincerely yours,
> Your Name

### My apartment promised security and there is none.
### "They may be responsible if you are injured."

*Dear Mr. Alderman:*

*I recently rented a new apartment. I chose one based on the agent's assurance that there was good security. In fact, there is none. All they have is a guard who never leaves his house at the entrance to the complex. I am concerned for my safety and want to know my rights.*

First, I should point out that apartments have no obligation to provide additional security. Basically, all the law requires is locks on doors and windows, lights in common areas, and fences and latches at pools.

A landlord may, however, be required to provide additional security in two instances. First, a landlord is responsible if he acts negligently. Negligence generally means not acting as a reasonable person would. For example, suppose that the landlord knows about a security problem, such as strangers walking around the complex, and takes no steps to either eliminate it or report it to the police. The landlord could be found to have acted negligently if he did not do what a reasonable person would have. If a reasonable person in the same position would have investigated, or hired security, or reported it to the police, the landlord's failure to act would be negligence.

The landlord may also be responsible under the Deceptive Trade Practices Act if he made any misrepresentations about security. This law, discussed in Chapter Ten, is a very powerful consumer protection law that also applies to renting apartments.

As far as I am concerned, if the agent told you there was good security, and there is none, the agent and the landlord have violated the Deceptive Trade Practices Act. This law would allow you to recover damages if you were injured as a result of the failure to provide the promised security, and it may also provide you with a basis to terminate your lease.

Your best bet may be to talk with the landlord and let him know you know about this law and expect the security you were promised. Hopefully you can negotiate a settlement you are happy with. You may not get security, but you may get him to agree to let you move out without breaching your lease.

### My landlord lied to me. What can I do?
### "The Texas Deceptive Trade Practices Act applies."

*Dear Mr. Alderman:*

*I just moved into a new apartment. When I looked at the model, the rental agent told me that when new tenants move in, the apartment is painted and the rugs are shampooed. I was scheduled to move in on Saturday and went to look at the unit on Wednesday. It had not even been cleaned, let alone painted. The agent again told me not to worry, that it would be painted by the time I moved in on Saturday. On Saturday, I arrived with my furniture and the unit was clean, but not painted. Also, the rugs were not shampooed. The owner had changed his mind and wasn't going to paint anymore. What are my rights?*

Any time someone leases anything, including an apartment, the Texas Deceptive Trade Practices Act applies. Under this law (discussed in Chapter Ten), it is unlawful to misrepresent the qualities or characteristics of something. For example, telling a tenant that an apartment will be painted when it will not be is a misrepresentation. As far as I am concerned, the landlord has violated the Deceptive Trade Practices Act by not providing an apartment as represented. I should also point out that because the agent is the authorized employee of the owner, the owner is liable for the agent's representations.

I suggest you reread Chapter Ten and then send the proper notice to the landlord demanding that your unit be painted and the rugs shampooed as promised or that you be reasonably compensated. A fair amount would be how much you are going to have to pay someone else to perform these services. If the landlord does not comply and you have to go to court to collect, the law entitles you to up to three times your damages plus any court costs and attorney's fees involved. As a practical matter, it is unlikely that you will end up in court. Usually, these problems are resolved once the other side knows that you know your rights.

### Can I sublease?
### "Not without consent."

*Dear Mr. Alderman:*

*I have a simple question to ask: Do I have the right to sublease my apartment? I have seven months left on my lease, and I am getting married. What I would like to do is sublease to a friend for the remainder of my lease term.*

You may not like this answer, but the law is clear: *You may not sublease unless your lease expressly gives you this right.* Under the law, a tenant does not have the right to sublease. This right can only be given to you by your landlord. I suggest that you read your lease carefully to see what it says about subleasing. If it is silent, then you do not have the right to sublease.

Even if your lease does not give you the right to sublease, your landlord may still agree to it. You should talk to him and try to get him to agree. You also should remember that even if he does agree, you will be responsible for the rent if your sub-tenant doesn't pay.

### Can my landlord just come in my apartment and take my property if I don't pay rent?
### "Maybe."

*Dear Mr. Alderman:*
*I admit it, I should pay my rent and it is my own fault that I was late, but does my landlord have the right to just come in and take my TV and stereo when I am late? I came home last night and there was a note telling me that as soon as I paid I could have the property back. I plan on paying the rent tomorrow but I want to know if what my landlord did was legal.*

The answer is, it is legal if all of the steps of the law have been followed. What your landlord is doing is asserting what is called a "landlord's lien." This allows the landlord to peacefully enter your apartment and take your property until you pay the rent. If you don't pay he has the right to sell the property. But to assert this lien certain requirements must be met.

First, the right to assert this lien must be underlined or printed in conspicuous bold print in your lease. Read your lease carefully; if the lien does not appear, the landlord has no right to take your property and doing so would, in effect, be theft, entitling you to substantial damages. Second, there is only certain property a landlord may take under this lien. Here is a list of what the law says the landlord *may not* take:

1. wearing apparel;
2. tools, apparatus, and books of a trade or profession;
3. schoolbooks;
4. a family library;

5. family portraits and pictures;
6. one couch, two living room chairs, and a dining table and chairs;
7. beds and bedding;
8. kitchen furniture and utensils;
9. food and foodstuffs;
10. medicine and medical supplies;
11. one automobile and one truck;
12. agricultural implements;
13. children's toys not commonly used by adults;
14. goods that the landlord or the landlord's agent knows are owned by a person other than the tenant or an occupant of the residence; and
15. goods that the landlord or the landlord's agent knows are subject to a recorded chattel mortgage or financing agreement.

If the landlord has taken any of this property he has violated the law. Finally, the landlord must leave you a note telling you what he took and what you need to do to get it back (the note must also tell you how much you owe in back rent). The bottom line is that, although a landlord may have the right to take your property pursuant to a landlord's lien, the requirements of the law are often not met and the landlord is acting wrongfully. If you feel your landlord has acted wrongfully, speak with him and try and get your property back. If you can't, you should consider small claims court or an attorney. Under the law, a landlord who violates the provision of the lien law is responsible for all the tenant's damages, and one month's rent, or $500, whichever is greater, plus attorneys' fees.

### My landlord has locked me out. Help!
### "There is a law."

*Dear Mr. Alderman:*
*I recently lost my job and got behind in my rent. Last night when I got home my landlord had changed the locks on the door of my apartment and told me to get off the property until I come up with some money. I don't have any way to get the money I owe him and I just want to get my things and leave. How long can he hold all of my property?*

Unless your landlord has a landlord's lien and acts according to state law (read the prior letter) he can't hold your property at all. *In fact, it is illegal for a landlord to just lock you out no matter how much money you owe.* Under the law a landlord has the right to change the locks on your doors but he must give you notice of where a key is and he must let you in whenever you want. He also can't stop you from removing your property and moving out. As I said before, only if he has a landlord's lien can he hold your property.

I suggest you talk with the landlord and let him know that you know the law. A landlord who illegally locks you out can be liable for substantial damages.

### Do I have to live in an apartment complex with children?
### "Yes, unless the complex is for persons over age 55."

*Dear Mr. Alderman:*
*I live in a very nice apartment complex just outside town. I have lived here for five years and it has always been "adult only." Recently, several families with children moved into the complex and the whole mood has changed. The complex is no longer the quiet place it once was. I am awakened on weekend mornings by the sound of motorized toys in the courtyard.*
*I complained to the management and they said there is nothing they can do; a new law requires that they rent to people with children. Is this the law? Don't I have the right to live where I want?*

Under recent amendments to the federal Fair Housing Act, it is illegal to discriminate against families with children with respect to housing. This means that a landlord must rent to anyone, regardless of whether they are married, single, or have children. The only restrictions that may be placed are those that apply to all. For example, the number of occupants per unit may be limited. It can't be limited, however, to adults.

There is a major exception to this law, however, that may help you. If a complex has 80% or more units occupied by at least one person over age 55, it is not required to take children. If you are over 55 it may be a good idea to look for one of the "seniors only" complexes. Seniors only is now another way of saying no children.

One last point. Just because apartments cannot discriminate against children or families with children does not mean you have to have your peace and quiet disturbed. If the children are getting up very early and making a lot of noise, the manager has the right to insist that they be kept quiet. I suggest you speak with the management and ask them to take steps to ensure that the children comply with the same rules and regulations as everyone else.

## I was refused an apartment because they said my wheelchair would ruin the carpet. Is this legal?
## "No. You can't discriminate against the handicapped."

*Dear Mr. Alderman:*
*I am handicapped, confined to a wheelchair. I recently found the perfect apartment and when I went to sign the lease was told by the landlord that I would have to look elsewhere. He told me, "Your wheelchair will ruin my carpet." Is this legal? I thought there were new laws protecting the handicapped. I realize my chair may do some damage but I am willing to pay for it.*

You are right. Recent amendments to the Fair Housing Act prohibit discrimination against a handicapped person. Handicap is defined to include a physical or mental impairment which substantially limits one or more of such person's major life activities.

Based on what you say, the landlord has acted illegally. Under the law he could be subject to civil penalties of up to $10,000. You can enforce this law privately, with the assistance of an attorney, or you can contact the Department of Housing and Urban Development. At a minimum, I would contact the landlord and let him know what the law is. Hopefully he was just uninformed and will now take steps to comply with the law.

## Can my landlord ask for more security deposit?
## "If it is a new lease, yes."

*Dear Mr. Alderman:*
*I live in an apartment and have a six-month lease. This is the third such lease I have signed. Every time a lease is up my landlord asks me to sign a new one. Each time I sign a new lease, however, my landlord raises my security deposit by $20. Is this legal?*

Yes. If you have a lease, the terms of your agreement with your landlord are governed by the lease and cannot be changed without your consent. In other words, during the lease period your security deposit could not be raised. When your lease expires, however, both you and the landlord are free to either renew the lease on its present terms, terminate the agreement, or write a new agreement.

For example, at the end of your lease, the rent could be raised or lowered, or the six-month term could be increased or decreased. Similarly, if your landlord wants additional security, he may ask for it. Of course, if you don't want to pay it you have the right to give notice and move. The amount of the security deposit is a matter to be negotiated by you and the landlord.

# CHAPTER THIRTEEN

# Mail-Order & Telephone Sales

MAIL-ORDER and telephone sales are big business. Today you can buy everything from food and clothing to furniture, from catalogs. You can shop in the privacy of your home or office, with no high-pressure salesperson looking over your shoulder. For the busy worker, catalogs and newspaper ads have replaced the department store.

But shopping at home has one big drawback: you don't see what you are buying and you don't receive it as soon as you pick it out. When you go into a store and buy a pair of jogging shoes, you pick out the style and size you want, try them on, pay for them, and off you go. You are on your way home to use them.

But when you buy the same pair of jogging shoes through the mail, you must first pay, and then wait until they arrive. And two bad things can happen: 1) they may never arrive; or 2) they may not be what you thought they were. These are the risks inherent in shopping by mail or over the phone; you must pay first and then wait for the goods—goods that you cannot examine until they arrive, if they arrive at all. However, the next few letters will show you that shopping by mail or phone does not have to be risky. There are laws to ensure that you can enjoy the convenience of shopping at home, *without* the risk of never receiving what you paid for.

**What can I do if the goods never arrive?**
**"Next time, use a credit card."**

*Dear Mr. Alderman:*
*I saw an ad in a magazine for a Wizard Roach Remover, guaranteed to keep roaches out of your house for two months. I sent the company $19.95 plus postage, over five weeks ago. I still have not received my roach killer, and the company won't answer my letters. They did cash my check, though. What can I do to get my money back? The company is in Iowa.*

I have some good news and some bad. The bad news is that you may be out of luck unless the company voluntarily sends you your money back. *The good news is that you can avoid this problem in the future by taking advantage of a federal law, the Fair Credit Billing Act.*

First, as to what you can do now. As the next letter discusses more fully, under the law a mail-order company can only wait 30 days to send you your goods. In your case they have already delayed beyond this period. The problem is that to enforce any of your rights against the company you will have to sue, and even if you used small claims court in Texas, you probably could not collect unless the company has assets or an office here. In other words, you are probably out of luck because it will cost you more to enforce your rights than you have lost in the deal. You may take steps to try to prevent this from happening to others by contacting the Better Business Bureau, the Federal Trade Commission, and the attorney general's office and telling them of your problem.

So what can you do to avoid this in the future? *Use a credit card whenever you order by mail.* Under the Fair Credit Billing Act, the credit card company cannot collect for items that you ordered but never received. If you had paid for your goods with a credit card you could simply contact the credit card company and tell them that there is a billing error and that you are not going to pay your bill. Here is what you should do to protect yourself.

## When the goods don't arrive:

When many consumers find a mistake on their bill, such as a charge for goods that never arrived, they pick up the phone and call the company to correct the problem. You can do this if you wish, but phoning does not trigger the legal safeguards provided under the law. To be protected under the Fair Credit Billing Act, you must send a separate *written* billing error notice to the credit card company. Your notice must reach the company within 60 days after the first bill containing the error was mailed to you. Send the notice to the address provided on the bill for billing error notices (and not, for example, directly to the store, unless the bill says that's where it should be sent). In your letter, you must include the following information: your name and account number; a statement that you believe the bill contains a billing error and the dollar amount involved; and the reasons why you believe there is a mistake— the goods never arrived. It's a good idea to send it by certified mail, return-receipt-requested. That way you'll have proof of the dates of mailing and receipt. If you wish, send photocopies of sales slips or other documents, but keep the originals for your records.

## What must the credit card company do?

Your letter claiming a billing error must be acknowledged by the credit card company within 30 days after it is received, unless the problem is resolved within that period. In any case, within two billing cycles (but not more than 90 days), the creditor must conduct a reasonable investigation and either correct the mistake or explain why the bill is believed to be correct.

## What happens while the credit card company investigates?

You may withhold payment of the amount in dispute, including the affected portions of minimum payments and finance charges, until the dispute is resolved. You are still required to pay any part of the bill that is not disputed, including finance and other charges on undisputed amounts.

While the Fair Credit Billing Act dispute settlement procedure is going on, the creditor may not take any legal or other action to collect the amount in dispute. Your account may not be closed or restricted in any way, except that the disputed amount may be applied against your credit limit.

## What happens once the credit card company determines you never received the goods?

If your bill is found to contain a billing error (the goods didn't arrive), the creditor must write you explaining the corrections to be made on your account. In addition to crediting your account with the amount not owed, the creditor must remove all finance charges, late fees, or other charges relating to that amount.

*The credit card company must follow these procedures or it will be violating federal law. If you feel the credit card company has not complied with the law, you should report it to the nearest Federal Trade Commission regional office, or to the Federal Trade Commission, Fair Credit Billing, Washington, D.C. 20580.*

## How long do I have to wait?
## "Thirty days."

*Dear Mr. Alderman:*
*Three months ago I ordered a new bathing suit. It cost over $30. I still have not received the suit and it is almost fall. The company keeps telling me that it will arrive any day. What can I do? I want my money back, not a bikini to wear in the winter.*

Under federal law a seller must deliver the goods within the time promised. If no time is stated in your agreement there is a presumption that 30 days is reasonable. *If your bathing suit has not arrived within 30 days, the company must notify you of when it will be delivered and let you cancel if you change your mind.*

Based on your letter, it appears the company has violated the law and you have the right to cancel and get your money back. I suggest that you write the company, once more, via certified mail, return-receipt-requested, and tell them you want to cancel your order. If you do not receive your money back, you should contact the Federal Trade Commission and tell them that the company has violated the mail-order rules.

You should also know that the company, by violating the federal law, may have violated the Texas Deceptive Trade Practices Act as well. This means that the attorney general could take action against the company and that you could file suit in small claims court for three times your damages. The problem with your filing suit is that the company is probably far away, and collecting anything will be very difficult.

So what can you do? Read the letter right before this one, and next time make sure you use a credit card.

## What happens when the wrong thing arrives?
## "Protect yourself."

*Dear Mr. Alderman:*
*I recently ordered a woman's size 12 jacket from a company in New York. It arrived three weeks later as a man's size 42. I sent it back to the company and they told me they would send a new one. They have*

*not sent a new jacket, and they have cashed my check for $50. What can I do? I don't think the company is even in business anymore.*

If you have read the letter right before this one you know that there is a federal law that requires companies to deliver goods, or give you a refund, within 30 days. The problem is that even though you are entitled to your jacket, or your money back, it will be very difficult, if not impossible, for you to collect. Having legal rights is meaningless unless the company you have rights against is solvent and in a location where it is convenient for you to sue.

So what do you do? First, report the company to the Federal Trade Commission for violating federal mail-order laws. Then, if the company has a local office, or owns property in Texas, you can sue in small claims court. From your letter, though, it sounds like the company has disappeared with your money, and now what you should be concerned about is making sure this never happens again.

In the future, to protect yourself, make sure you use a credit card whenever you order by mail. Then if you don't receive what you ordered, the Fair Credit Billing Act lets you withhold payment from the credit card company. To find out just how this law works, read the letter on page 132.

### I didn't order this. What can I do?
### "Accept the gift."

*Dear Mr. Alderman:*
*The other day I arrived home and found a box on my doorstep. It was from a company in Nebraska that I had never heard of. Inside was all sorts of junk: toys, stationery, ashtrays, and trinkets. The letter that came with the stuff said that it was sent to me on approval and that I could keep it for only $49.95, or send it back. The post office wants five bucks to send the junk back and I don't want to pay it. It doesn't seem right that I get stuck because of this stupid company. Is there anything that I can do?*

You are in luck. Texas and federal law provide that you may treat unsolicited merchandise as a gift. *If you did not order the goods* (but be careful, because you may have signed something a long time ago agreeing to accept such orders on approval), *you can do whatever you want with them.* I think that to be polite you should write the company a letter and thank them for the gift and tell them that you will be glad to receive other gifts from them in the future. If you do not want to keep the merchandise, you may want to tell the company that if they will send you postage you will return it. Of course, if you want, you can simply throw the box away.

The only requirement that must be met before the goods can be treated as a gift is that it must not be ordered or solicited by you. To make sure that you didn't order them, you may want to write the company via certified mail, return-receipt, and ask for proof that you ordered the goods. You should tell the company that unless it can show you that you did in fact order the goods, you will keep them as you are permitted to do by law.

The Texas law is a short one so I thought I would let you see what it says:

Unless otherwise agreed, where unsolicited goods are delivered to a person, he has a right to refuse to accept delivery of the goods and is not bound to return such goods to the sender. Goods received due to a bonafide mistake are to be returned, but the burden of proof of the error shall be upon the sender. If such unsolicited goods are either addressed to or intended for the recipient, they shall be deemed a gift to the recipient, who may use them or dispose of them in any manner without any obligation to the sender. Provided, however, the provisions of this Act shall not apply to goods substituted for goods ordered or solicited by the recipient.

*Remember: This law applies only to unsolicited merchandise. If you authorize a company to send you merchandise on approval, such as with a book club, you do not have the right to keep it and you must bear the cost of returning the item.*

# CHAPTER FOURTEEN

# Neighborly Problems

MOST of us get along well with our neighbors, and if a dispute arises we settle it by talking it out and reaching a fair compromise. But
sometimes you can have a problem with your neighbor that you just can't
settle—and then knowing your legal rights can help you decide what step
to take next.

*The best advice I can ever give is to try to settle your disputes in a
friendly way. The law is designed to help in those situations where the parties themselves can't work it out. Remember, you might be neighbors for a
long time. Compromise is the key when dealing with your neighbors.*

### My neighbor's tree fell on my car. Who's responsible?
### "Why did the tree fall?"

*Dear Mr. Alderman:*
*Last week there was a severe thunderstorm. The wind blew down my
neighbor's tree, and part of the tree landed on my car. The damage
to my car will cost approximately $1500 to repair. I have insurance
but it has a $500 deductible. I have talked with my neighbor, but he
refuses to pay and says that it wasn't his fault. Do I have any rights?
Can I force him to pay?*

Your neighbor may not have to pay for the damage to your car, even
though it was his tree. *Under the law your neighbor is only responsible
to you if he was negligent in caring for the tree.* In other words, if the tree
was healthy and blew down in an unusually strong wind, your neighbor
would probably not have any liability. But, if the tree was diseased, and
your neighbor knew it, he could be responsible for the damage if the tree
fell during a regular storm, one that did not blow over healthy trees.

People owe a duty to their neighbors to keep their property in a way
that will not injure their neighbors. If your neighbor was negligent in the
care of his property, he is responsible for the damage caused. But your

neighbor is not responsible for an "act of God" that could not have been prevented, even by the most careful person.

### What can I do about my neighbor's tree?
### "Trim it carefully."

*Dear Mr. Alderman:*
*My neighbor's tree hangs over my garage and is very close to the roof. I am afraid that a strong wind will blow the tree onto my property and damage it. Do I have the right to cut the overhanging branches down? Can I force my neighbor to cut it? Who will be responsible if the tree damages my property?*

Problems with neighbor's trees can be among the most difficult to resolve, both legally and practically. Because the tree is on your neighbor's property, you do not have the right to cut it down. You may have the right to cut the overhanging branches; however, if you injure the tree, you could be responsible. The best suggestion may be to speak with your neighbor and let him know about the problem. Explain that the branches are a hazard to your property and that you would like him to cut them down. If you are willing to do it, tell him so. If he still refuses to work with you, he could be liable for any damage that occurs. As I said in the previous letter, the owner of a tree is negligent, and therefore responsible, if he does not take reasonable steps to protect you and your property from harm. In my opinion, not cutting overhanging branches after being warned of a danger is negligence.

### What happens if the neighbor's kid is hurt playing in my yard?
### "You are probably not responsible."

*Dear Mr. Alderman:*
*I don't want to sound like someone who doesn't like kids—I do—but the neighbor's children are worrying me. They seem to find my roof an exciting place to play, and just last week, I caught two 9-year-olds up on the roof. They climb up from the fence and then wander around wherever they like. What I need to know is whether I am in trouble if they get hurt up there. I have done everything I can do to stop them, but they keep coming back.*

If you have done everything a reasonable person would do to keep the children off your roof, then you probably will not be responsible if one of the children is injured. *The law only imposes a duty on you to take ordinary care to protect the trespassing children from injury.* This means taking reasonable steps to keep them off your property, and not leaving unusually dangerous conditions where the children play.

For example, if the children climb over a fence to get to your property, you probably are not responsible if they fall and injure themselves. But if you were to leave a gun outside, where you knew the children played, you could be responsible if one of them was shot. The test is what would a reasonable person do in a similar situation.

There is one exception to this general rule that you should know about. There is a doctrine known as "attractive nuisance," which places a greater duty on a landowner when there is a condition known to be attractive to children. For example, we all know that children like swimming pools. If you have a pool in your yard the law presumes that you know children will try to use it and imposes an obligation on you to take extra steps to keep them out. While a person generally does not have a duty to fence his property to keep out trespassers, an owner with a pool may be required to do so.

### Do I have to pay for damage caused by my child? "As a legal matter, no."

*Dear Mr. Alderman*
*Recently my son and some of his friends were playing baseball in the lot near our house. I am not sure exactly what happened, but somehow my son threw a baseball through our neighbor's window. Now my neighbor has insisted that I pay for it. I intend to pay to be a good neighbor, but I was wondering what my legal liability would be if I didn't?*

As far as the law is concerned, you probably are not liable. Generally, parents are not responsible for wrongs committed by their children. There are, however, a few exceptions.

First, you would be responsible if the accident occurred as a result of your failure to properly supervise your child. For example, if the kids were playing in the backyard, and you did not take reasonable steps to make sure they hit the ball away from windows, instead of toward them, you could liable. Under the law, parents are also responsible for willful and malicious acts committed by a child between the ages of 12 and 18. If your child intentionally threw the ball at the window, and he was between the ages of 12 and 18, you would be responsible under this law.

*The bottom line, however, is that your decision to pay is probably the best one. Sometimes being a good neighbor is more important than exercising your legal rights.*

### How can I stop my neighbor's barking dog? "There may be a law."

*Dear Mr. Alderman:*
*Why is it the smallest dogs seem to make the most noise? My neighbor has a small dog that barks all day when she is gone. My neighbor leaves the dog outside and it stands at my fence and barks. It is driving me crazy. This would be bad enough but she lets the dog out every morning at 6:00 A.M. When the dog wants back in, about five minutes later, it just starts barking. I have talked to my neighbor and she says there is nothing she can do—dogs will be dogs. I don't want to get into an argument with her about who is right and who is wrong until I know my rights. Does a neighbor have the right to force someone to stop their dog from barking like this?*

I have been surprised by the number of people who have written me about barking dogs—and unfortunately I don't have a simple answer. There are, however, two areas of law that may help you.

Under general legal principles you cannot use your property, or maintain it, in a manner that is a nuisance to others. If the barking dog is seriously disrupting your enjoyment of your property, you may be able to sue your neighbor to force her to stop. The test, however, would be whether a reasonable person would be seriously disturbed by the dog. For example, if the dog barked occasionally during the day, something all dogs do, you probably would not have any basis for objection. On the other hand, if it barked all night, your neighbor would probably be maintaining a nuisance. If the dog is a nuisance you can bring a lawsuit to stop it.

Before you consider a lawsuit, though, you should see if there are any local laws or ordinances directly on point. The first thing I suggest you do is contact your local governing body. Many cities and counties have laws regulating barking dogs and you could get them to enforce the law. If there are no specific laws or ordinances, then you will have to bring a civil action, a costly and often time-consuming thing to do.

*The best advice I can give you is to try to talk to your neighbor and work it out. You may be right legally, but it will be very difficult to prove and enforce.*

## The neighbor's dog bit me. Must the neighbor pay? "It depends."

*Dear Mr. Alderman:*
*My neighbor has a large, vicious dog. The dog is always chasing my children and has bitten one of them before. Last week the dog got out of his fence and bit my son, doing severe damage. The doctor bills were very expensive, and our insurance didn't cover them. I have asked my neighbor to pay the bills and he said no. I told him I would sue and he said "go ahead, an owner isn't legally responsible for what a dog does." Is this true? How can a person let his dog bite people and not have to pay the bills?*

Based on what you say in your letter I think your neighbor is wrong. In some states a pet owner is "strictly liable" for injuries caused by a pet. This means that if a dog bites someone, the owner must pay for the damages regardless of whether the owner did anything wrong. Unfortunately, Texas has not yet adopted a rule like this, and in Texas you must show that the owner was "negligent." That is, the owner had reason to know the dog would bite and didn't take reasonable steps to protect you. In many cases this means that the dog must have either bitten someone previously or be known to have vicious tendencies.

In your case the dog had chased and bitten people before and the owner should have known the dog was vicious. If the owner did not take reasonable steps to protect you, for example, by keeping the dog well penned, I believe the owner should be responsible. If the amount is low enough for you to go to small claims court (see Chapter Fifteen) you can sue without an attorney.

One final point. In many cases the breed of dog, for example, a pit bull, is known to be vicious. In my opinion, owners of this kind of dog are held to a higher standard and should be responsible when the dog bites, even if the dog never bit before. While the owner of a poodle may not have to take steps to protect you from injury, the law probably imposes a higher duty on the owner of a dog whose breed is known to be vicious.

### My neighbor's dog got my dog pregnant.
### Is my neighbor responsible?
### "Yes, owners are responsible for the consequences of their dog's act."

*Dear Mr. Alderman:*
*I have a very strange problem. I recently came home to find my neighbor's dog engaged in intercourse with my dog in my backyard. My dog is chained up in our fenced backyard. My neighbor's dog had been running loose and dug under my fence. My dog is a pedigree, and we want to breed her. To protect our dog, and to not have to deal with a litter of mutt puppies, we terminated the pregnancy. I asked my neighbor to help pay the costs, and he refused, saying he was not responsible for the misdeeds of his dog. Is he?*

Don't think your problem is that strange, or that unusual. These things do happen. In fact, in a recent case in Florida the owner of a Rottweiler successfully sued the owner of a Chihuahua for impregnating his dog under similar circumstances.

As far as I am concerned, your neighbor should be responsible if he did not take proper steps to insure that his dog did not run wild and break into your yard. If your city has a leash law that was broken, your neighbor should be responsible for not complying with this law. If there is no such law, you must show that your neighbor knew that his dog was running wild and that there was a likelihood that he would take advantage of other dogs in heat. Generally, owners are responsible for conduct such as you describe.

I should point out, however, that the neighbor may not be responsible if he had done everything he could to keep the dog locked up, and it was not his fault that the dog got out. For example, if the dog was locked in the backyard and someone else opened the gate and let the dog out, your neighbor probably would not be responsible.

Finally, as you might guess, it can be very hard to prove the case of the promiscuous poodle. The best advice may be to speak with your neighbor again and try to work things out.

### My car was vandalized at a restaurant.
### Is the restaurant responsible?
### "It depends."

*Dear Mr. Alderman:*
*The other night, I went to dinner with my boyfriend. We parked the*
*car in front of the restaurant and when we came out we found that*
*the front window had been smashed and the tape deck stolen. We*
*talked to the manager of the restaurant and he said that the restau-*
*rant was not responsible. Is that true? It doesn't seem right. They*
*provide the parking lot. Don't they have to provide security?*

There is no simple answer to your question. Legally, the restaurant is
only liable if it has been negligent. That is, if it did not take reasonable
care to protect your property. For example, ordinarily, a restaurant does
not have to provide security. This means that if there is an incident of vandalism, the restaurant probably would not be responsible. But once a
restaurant (or any other establishment, for that matter) knows that there
may be problems, or that it is located in a high-crime area, its obligations
change. Now the restaurant must take reasonable steps to protect its customers. If it does not, it will be responsible. For example, if every restaurant in that neighborhood had lights and security guards in the parking lot
and this restaurant did not, it probably would be liable because it was negligent. On the other hand, if it does the same thing as everyone else has
done to protect you and vandalism still occurs, it probably is not liable.

Simply because your property is damaged while it is in a parking lot is
not enough to make the owner responsible. To recover, you will have to
show that they did not take reasonable steps to protect your property.
What is reasonable will depend on how high the risk of vandalism is,
how much knowledge the owner has of the risk, and what others do
under similar circumstances. If you feel an owner did not act reasonably
to protect you, you should consider a claim for negligence in small
claims court.

### My stolen property ended up in a pawn shop. Can I get it back?
### "Yes!"

*Dear Mr. Alderman:*
*I was robbed. The thief took all my jewelry and electronic equip-*
*ment. Now I have found out that they caught him and know where he*
*pawned my property. Can I get my property back from the pawn*
*shop? What if it has been sold? It seems like this is my property and*
*I ought to be entitled to it.*

You are right. It is your property and under the law, you can get it back from whomever has it. If a thief steals your property, anyone who receives it is subject to your title. This means that the pawnbroker, or anyone who purchased it from the pawnbroker, will have to return it to you. Of course, you will have to prove that the property is yours. That is why it is a good idea to keep serial numbers and photographs of all your valuables.

### The apartment next door has an unfenced pool. What can I do? "There is a new law."

*Dear Mr. Alderman:*
*We live very close to a small apartment complex. The apartment has a swimming pool in the middle of the complex. It does not have a fence and the door to the courtyard is always open. I am afraid that my young son will play in the pool and drown. What can I do to get them to fence in the pool? I have checked with the city, and they say it is within city building codes.*

In 1993 the Texas legislature enacted a law governing swimming pool enclosures. Under this law, pools that are owned by an apartment complex or a property owners' association must be properly enclosed. Basically, to comply with this law, a pool must have a fence around it at least 48 inches high. It also must have a gate that is self-closing and self-latching.

This law may be privately enforced by a tenant, a homeowner, or any other interested party. Many government agencies, including the attorney general's office, the local health department, and the city or county attorney's office, also can bring an action to enforce it. If the apartment has not taken steps to comply with the new law, I suggest you speak with them and then contact the appropriate official to have them require compliance. I should point out that failure to comply could result in civil penalties of up to $5,000.

# CHAPTER FIFTEEN

# Small Claims Court

KNOWING your legal rights is just the beginning. To make this knowledge work for you, you must be able to assert them. Small claims court fills this need. It is inexpensive, simple to use, and can promptly settle disputes. Small claims court is where you put your knowledge to work.

As I said in the introduction, once you know your legal rights, you usually will not have to pursue a legal claim. The other party will try to settle the problem. But sometimes a dispute cannot be settled and you must resort to the legal system to resolve it.

*The decision of whether or not to sue must be made by you, based on the amount of money involved, the importance of the issues, and how much time and expense you are willing to spend to pursue your claim. Don't let emotion reign over common sense. You are always better off trying to settle with the other party before you go to court. But if you cannot settle, small claims court gives you a chance to appear before a judge or jury and have an impartial tribunal decide who is correct.*

As you will see from the following letters, small claims court is relatively easy to use and very inexpensive. Also, if you are successful you will be awarded the costs of the lawsuit in addition to your other damages.

Many people ask me: "Is small claims court in Texas like 'People's Court' on TV?" The best answer I can give to that question is what a small claims court judge told me when I asked him how his court compared with the TV court. His answer: "We are a lot like the People's Court—just much less formal."

### How much can I sue for in small claims court?
### "Up to $5,000!"

*Dear Mr. Alderman:*
*I heard that there was a change in the law and that I can now sue for more than $1,000 in small claims court.*

Good news. Yes! The legislature amended the law and now the limit in small claims court is $5,000.

I should point out that this makes small claims court much more useful for the Deceptive Trade Practices Act. As I explained on pages 103–104, if you win under this law and your damages are less than $1,000, you automatically get three times that amount. For example, if you sue and win $200 the court must award you $600. For suits over $1,000, you can get three times your damages if you prove the person acted "knowingly." Because of this trebling, some believe that suits under the Deceptive Trade Practices Act cannot be brought in small claims court if the amount, when trebled, is over the court's limit. Now, with the higher limit, you can allege that the person acted "knowingly," sue for up to $1,666.67, and still get three times your damages. Small claims court in Texas is really becoming a "people's court."

### How do I sue in small claims court?
### "It's easy."

*Dear Mr. Alderman:*
*My laundry man is incompetent! The other day I brought in a brand new shirt that I had only worn once, and he ruined it. It has grease all over it, and even though I had only worn it once, the owner said it must have been my fault. Having worn it only to the movies, there was no way I could have gotten grease all over it. My friend who was with me saw that the shirt was clean when I left the movies. Now I am mad! I want to sue, but I am afraid the cleaners will have a big-time lawyer, and I will lose. Do I need an attorney? The shirt only cost $25. Is it worth it?*

Small claims court is designed for you. Your claim can be quickly decided by the court based upon the information you give the judge. You will not need a lawyer. If you can prove that the shirt did not have grease stains on it when you brought it to the laundry and that the laundry stained it, you will be entitled to the value of the shirt, plus the amount it costs you to bring the suit.

*Suing in small claims court is easy. However, in order to sue in this court, you must be asking for no more than $5,000.* In small claims court, you can sue any person who is actually in Texas, or has a permanent home in Texas, or is doing business here. To sue a sole proprietorship, the proprietor must be in Texas; to sue a partnership, the partners must be here; and to sue a corporation, it must do business in the state. For more information on what it means to do business in one of these forms, read Chapter Thirteen.

There are many small claims courts, so after you decide to go to small claims court, you must find the proper location for your complaint. Generally, you must sue in the court that covers the area where the person you are suing lives or where the business operates, or where the transaction took place. Small claims courts are part of the justice courts, so look in the phone book for the justice of the peace in that area. If you have any questions about which court to sue in or whom you can sue, call and ask the clerk of the court. The clerk will be able to answer your question.

After you know which court to go to, go to that court and tell the clerk that you want to sue the laundry. *Make sure that you have the correct name and address of the laundry and, if you can find it, the name of a person at the laundry who can be served with the legal papers.* If the laundry is a corporation, you can call the secretary of state in Austin and find out who the laundry's *agent for service* is. An *agent for service* is the person the company has designated to accept legal papers for the corporation.

When you get to the court, the clerk will give you a *petition* to fill out. Read it carefully. If you have any questions, ask the clerk. A typical small claims court petition is shown on page 149.

You, the person suing, are called the *plaintiff.* You start the lawsuit by filing a *petition.* After you file the petition and pay your fees (about $55), the court will have the constable or sheriff serve the *defendant,* the person or business being sued, with the papers. The defendant will then either *answer* your claim (that is, state why he thinks he is not responsible) or *default* (that is, not respond to the petition). If the defendant does not respond to the petition, you will go before the judge, and tell him or her what your claim is. If you have a case, you will win. The judge will award you the amount of your shirt plus what it cost for you to sue. *Make sure that you ask for all of the costs of bringing the suit in your petition.*

If the defendant answers your claim, he will be present in the courtroom on the date set for the trial. Unless either party asks for a jury, the case will be heard by the judge alone. In most cases, the hearing is very informal. The judge lets both sides tell their story and listens to any other witnesses that may appear. For example, if your friend knows that the shirt was not stained when you brought it in, you may want to bring him with you to court to tell this to the judge. Also, if you have any pictures or other records that support your case, you should bring them with you.

Typical small claims court petition.

---

### In the Small Claims Court of _____ County, Texas

Plaintiff

vs.

Defendant

State of Texas

County of _____

(Plaintiff), whose post office address is

_____

Street and Number

_____ , _____

City                                              County,

Texas, being duly sworn, on his oath deposes and says that (defendant), whose post office address is       _____

_____ , _____

County, Texas, is justly indebted to him in the sum of _____ Dollars and _____ Cents ($ _____ ), for _____

_____

_____

(here the nature of the claim should be stated in concise form and without technicality, including all pertinent dates), and that there are no counter claims existing in favor of the defendant and against the plaintiff, except _____

_____

_____

Plaintiff

Subscribed and sworn to before me this _____ day of _____ ,

19___.

_____

Judge

---

The sales receipt showing that the shirt was new may be important. And, of course, bring the shirt to show the judge the damage.

If the other side has a lawyer, don't worry about being intimidated. Most judges will limit what a lawyer may do. Small claims court is a people's court. Most judges will ensure that you are treated fairly and have a chance to tell your side of the story.

After hearing all the evidence, the judge will usually make a prompt ruling and state who wins. Usually that is the end of the matter. If you win, the other side pays you the money. But sometimes it can be difficult to collect your judgment, as the letter on pages 151–152 shows.

### What happens if I sue for more than $5,000 in small claims court? "You will be thrown out of court."

*Dear Mr. Alderman:*

*I recently did some contracting work for someone. They asked me to do a small job first, and then another, and then another. They now owe me $6,200. I have tried to get them to pay, but it looks like I am going to have to sue. I recently read that you can only sue for $5,000 in small claims court. I would be satisfied to get this much out of them, and I don't want to have to get a lawyer to sue for more. Can I just take the $5,000 and call it even?*

No. If you file a suit in small claims court asking for more than $5,000, the court does not have jurisdiction. This means that it does not have legal authority to hear your case and will have to dismiss it. You are not allowed to simply "take less" to get into small claims court. If you want to sue for more than $5,000, you will have to file in district or county court. This will probably mean hiring an attorney. But there is another alternative for you.

Although you cannot sue for a total of more than $5,000, when there are several contracts you can sue separately for each. For example, you said that you did more than one job. As far as the law is concerned, each job is a separate contract and you can file a separate suit for each. As long as each job was less than $5,000, the court has jurisdiction to hear the case. This will cost you a little more in filing fees, but you recover these fees if you win.

One final point. Do not try to get into court by reducing your damages. If you are owed $5,800, you cannot just sue for $5,000 to get into small claims court. The amount in controversy is over $5,000 and the court will dismiss the case.

### Can I just take less to get into small claims court?
### "No!"

*Dear Mr. Alderman:*
*I am owed $5,700 on a debt. I know you can only sue for up to*
*$5,000 in Small Claims Court. Can I sue in Small Claims Court if I*
*am willing to accept $5,000 for what I am owed?*

Basically the answer is no. As you correctly state, Small Claims Court jurisdiction is $5,000. This means that it cannot hear cases involving disputes in excess of that amount. In your case your dispute involves $5,700. Even though you are willing to accept $5,000, you have no legal basis to sue for anything less than $5,700. This means that Small Claims Court would not have jurisdiction to hear your case. You should consider a suit in either County or District Court. You will probably need an attorney to assist you with this claim.

### What do I do after I've won?
### "Execute your judgment."

*Dear Mr. Alderman:*
*You may remember me: I am the person who wrote to you about a*
*problem with my cleaner. Well, I took your advice and went to small*
*claims court—and I won! Now, what do I do? He won't pay and I*
*still don't have my money.*

If you win in small claims court, the person you sued will usually pay you the money he or she owes you immediately. However, if you have difficulty collecting your judgment, the law can help you.

The first thing you should do is write the defendant and remind him that you have been awarded a judgment against him. Ask him to pay you the money he owes you. If he still refuses to pay you, there are some things you can do with the law's help.

There are two legal devices that you can use to force payment of your judgment. One is called an *abstract of judgment;* the other is a *writ of execution.* An abstract of judgment is a legal paper you can file that will give you a lien on any real estate, except for a homestead, owned by the defendant. To do this, you must go back to the court where you sued. The clerk will help you get the abstract of judgment. Then you must file it in every county where you think that the defendant may own real property.

There will be a small charge to do this but you will be entitled to collect this amount from the defendant. Once you file the abstract, you will have a lien against the defendant's non-exempt real property. This means that the defendant will probably not be able to sell the property without first paying you. You also will have the right to force him to sell the property to satisfy your judgment. Most people do not like to have liens on their property and will pay you to get the lien released.

The other method to force payment is called a writ of execution. This is also issued by the court where you got your judgment. It is an order to the sheriff or constable directing him to go to the defendant and collect the judgment. If the defendant still does not pay, the sheriff or constable has the right to take the defendant's non-exempt personal property and sell it in order to pay you your money. There may be a small cost for the writ and the services of the law officer, but this is recoverable from the defendant.

*Remember, if you are having trouble collecting your judgment, go back to the court clerk and ask for help. The clerk will tell you how to enforce your judgment.*

There is one last thing you should keep in mind. Texas law is very favorable to debtors. It is very difficult to force people to pay their debts if they really do not want to. For an abstract of judgment to be successfully enforced, the defendant must own real estate other than a homestead. To successfully collect your money with a writ of execution, the defendant must own property which is not exempted from collection by Texas law. The exemption law in Texas allows a person to keep most of his or her property no matter how much he or she owes. *Read the letter beginning on page 51 to see what property is exempt before you try to collect your judgment with a writ of execution.*

Before taking the time to try to collect your judgment, consider whether it will be worth the time and the effort you will have to put in. While you can usually force a business to pay, be aware that it is much more difficult to force individuals to pay a judgment.

### What is garnishment?
### "Another way to get your money."

*Dear Mr. Alderman:*
*I sued and won in small claims court. Now the person I sued is refusing to pay. A friend told me that if I knew where he banked I could use garnishment. What is this, and how do I use it?*

Garnishment is the name given to the proceeding that allows you to get money that is owed to the person you sued. It can be used to get money in a bank account, rent owed to landlords, or debts owed to individuals or businesses.

In some cases, garnishment may be used to get a portion of a person's wages. Wage garnishment is permitted in Texas only for the collection of child support, back taxes, and certain government-backed student loans. For debts other than these, wages are protected, and garnishment cannot be used to get money from someone who pays wages to the person you sued. But money owed to people who are self-employed, such as an independent contractor, a builder, an accountant, or an attorney, is not considered "wages," therefore, you may use garnishment to reach money owed to these individuals.

To use garnishment you should go back to the court and file a "writ of garnishment." To do this, you must have the name and address of the garnishee—the person who is holding the money you want. For example, suppose you know where the person you sued has a bank account. Under the law, the bank technically "owes" the money to the owner of the account. Therefore, you can use a writ of garnishment to order the bank to pay the money over to you to satisfy the debt.

Garnishment is not necessarily a complicated procedure; however, you may want to consult an attorney to help you with it. If you were to make a mistake, it could result in liability to you.

### Does a corporation have to have an attorney to go to small claims court? "No."

*Dear Mr. Alderman:*

*I am the president of a small corporation. We are owed money by several of our customers and I want to go to small claims court. A friend told me that a corporation can only go to court if it is represented by an attorney. Is this true? It will cost me more to hire an attorney than the amount of the claims.*

Generally, your friend is correct. A corporation can only appear in court or file legal papers through an attorney. This is because the law treats a corporation as a separate legal entity and, as a separate entity, it must act through a representative. The only type of representative that can go to court is an attorney. If someone else went to court, they would be guilty of practicing law without a license.

But there is one important exception. A corporation may be represented in *small claims court* by any authorized agent. The legislature recognized that much of what goes on in small claims court is too simple to require the additional expense of an attorney. Therefore, you, as president of the corporation, may file the claim on behalf of the corporation.

# CHAPTER SIXTEEN

# Starting a Business

Each year, thousands of brave entrepreneurs venture out into the world of business. Some achieve a measure of fame and fortune while most discover the harsh realities of the small business: few are successful.

When you start a new business you suddenly find yourself on the "other side" of the law. To protect yourself it is important to know all of the laws that govern your business, and to make sure that you comply with them. But no matter how diligent and conscientious you may be, things can still go wrong and you may find yourself being sued by one of your customers.

For example, even if you did not know about the leak in your refrigerator, you may still incur substantial liability when someone slips and falls on the wet floor. And even though the product you sold was manufactured by someone else, you may be responsible when it explodes and injures someone.

There are three ways to avoid liability when you operate a business.

First:
Be careful to make sure you comply with the law.
Second:
Purchase enough insurance to cover any unexpected liability, such as the patron who slips and falls on a banana peel.
Third:
Consider incorporating. A business may be run as a sole proprietorship, a partnership, or a corporation. As you will see from the next few letters, the legal form your business assumes can determine the extent of *your* liability.

### What is a sole proprietorship?
### "The same thing as yourself."

*Dear Mr. Alderman:*
*I just opened up a little fix-it shop in my garage. I put up a sign that reads: "Sam's Fix It." So far I am not getting rich, but I am making*

*enough extra money to make it worthwhile. The other day someone brought in a toaster that needed to be repaired. I fixed it and returned it. Today they came back. The toaster had caught on fire. I had apparently crossed two wires that shouldn't be crossed. The owner was pretty nice about it and told me I was lucky his house hadn't burned down. Then I started thinking . . . What if the house had caught on fire because of my mistake? Who is responsible for things from my shop that go wrong?*

The simple answer to your question is: "You are." When you run a business as a sole proprietorship, you are the business. Whatever debts or obligations are incurred by the business are actually incurred by you. The business is not a separate entity. Perhaps the best way to look at it is that the business is just another name that you are using.

Many people start up a business by simply assuming a name and opening shop. While this is legal (of course you must file the assumed name with the county clerk), it may not be the best form for you. For example, if you didn't properly repair the toaster and it caught the house on fire, you may have had a substantial lawsuit to contend with. Even though you were acting as a business when you repaired the toaster, you would have personal liability for the damages caused. This means that you could lose personal *and* business assets to pay the debt.

As you will see from the next few letters, you may want to consider incorporating. A corporation is a separate entity. You are usually not personally liable for the obligation of the corporation. *Of course, no matter what form your business takes, you should make sure you have adequate liability insurance.*

**Who is responsible for partnership debts?
"All the partners."**

*Dear Mr. Alderman:*
*I have two partners in a small restaurant. One of them has gone crazy. He thinks we're the Ritz and has started buying caviar and all sorts of expensive junk. Most of the food goes bad, because no one orders it. The other day, we got the bills for all this stuff and we were shocked. There is no way we can pay for all the stuff he bought and still stay in business. We are now talking about splitting up and closing the restaurant, but I am worried about what my share of the bills might be. Do I have to pay a third of everything we owe?*

I have some bad news for you. You are not liable for one-third of the debts your partners have incurred. *You are responsible for all of the debts if they are not paid by the partnership.* Basically, each partner has full liability for all of the partnership debts. Each partner, however, has the right to recover from the others his fair share.

Here is how the law works:

Suppose A, B, and C form the ABC partnership. Each partner contributes $5,000. The business then incurs $21,000 in debts. The partnership assets will first be used to pay the debt. The remaining $6,000 is now owed by the partners. Each is responsible for $2,000, but if one doesn't pay, the others must pay his share. For example, if a creditor sues all the partners, but only A has any money, A will have to pay the entire $6,000. He will be responsible for getting $2,000 each from B and C.

Remember, a partnership is not a separate legal entity when it comes to liability. It is simply a way for more than one person to do business jointly. As far as the law is concerned, each partner is usually liable for whatever the partnership does. This can even include wrongful acts of the other partners, such as an automobile injury that occurs while making a delivery.

*If you are concerned with your individual liability for the debts of the business, don't use a partnership. Read the following letters and set up a limited partnership or a corporation.* But first, consider the partnership's liability for the personal debts of the partners.

### Can my partner's creditors take partnership property for his private debts?
### "No, partnerships generally are not liable for personal debts of the partners."

*Dear Mr. Alderman:*
*I recently set up a partnership with my friend Bob. We have a small business with about $5,000 in parts. Recently, the bank that loaned Bob money to build a pool at his house came and told us that if Bob didn't pay they would sue and take the property of the partnership. Can they do this? The business didn't borrow the money, Bob borrowed it himself. Our business is going along OK and I wouldn't want to have to end it.*

It is tempting here to go into a lot of law about liability and partnerships. But the simple answer is that your partner's creditors cannot force you to sell the partnership or take partnership assets. The partnership is not responsible for the personal debts of the individual partners. Of course, your partner's creditors can take your partner's interest in the business, and receive his share of the profits, to pay off the debt, but this should not affect the running of the business.

Partners are responsible for partnership debts and personal assets may be taken to pay them off, but the reverse is not true. A creditor of an individual partner may not take partnership property.

### What is a limited partnership?
### "A cross between a partnership and a corporation."

*Dear Mr. Alderman:*
*I am about to start a business with some friends. We have considered a partnership or a corporation, but recently someone told us there is such a thing as a limited partnership. We were told this is just like a partnership but without the liability. Because we are worried about our individual liability if we start a partnership, this sounds like a good idea. How does it work? Would you suggest we start one?*

You are right, a limited partnership is like a partnership but with limited liability. For example, if you start a partnership, you, and each of the partners, are responsible for all the debts of the partnership. As I said in the letter beginning on page 156, you, as a partner, could end up losing your personal property to pay off the partnership debts.

In a limited partnership, the limited partners are only responsible for an amount equal to their investment in the business. For example, if you were a limited partner with a $5,000 investment, the most you could lose would be the $5,000 you put in. But there are two big drawbacks to a limited partnership: there must be at least one general partner, who has individual liability for all the partnership debts; and, as a limited partner, you cannot be directly involved in the day-to-day running of the business. A limited partner is really a "silent partner." He invests in the business and then hopes that it succeeds so that he can share in the profits. From your letter it doesn't sound like a limited partnership is what you are looking for. You seem to want to be actively involved in the business, and a limited partner cannot be.

But just in case you do decide to start a limited partnership I should tell you that unlike a regular partnership, which can be started with only a handshake, a limited partnership is created by law and needs a formal agreement to be valid. To start a limited partnership you should consult with an attorney and have him or her draw up the papers.

### Is there a way to avoid liability?
### "Form a corporation."

*Dear Mr. Alderman:*
*I am going to open a small "Fruit Stand/Cheese Shop." I just read about a restaurant owner who was sued for over $100,000 by someone who slipped on a banana peel in his store. I am worried about this happening to me. I know that my insurance will cover most damage claims, but I really don't want to be held responsible for all the obligations of the business. Is there some way that the business can be responsible for its own debts?*

*One way for an individual to avoid liability for debts incurred by his business is to incorporate.* Under the law a corporation is a separate legal being. It sues and is sued in its own name. The individuals involved in a corporation can only lose their investment in the business.

For example, suppose you start your business as a sole proprietorship, and a customer is injured slipping on your floor. She sues for $150,000, not an unusually high amount these days. You lose, and your insurance pays $100,000. *You are personally responsible for the remaining $50,000.* The same result would occur if the business were a partnership.

But if you had incorporated, the business, not you, would owe the remaining $50,000. If the business didn't have enough money to pay the debt, the customer could not collect from you. If the business were to stop doing business, or file bankruptcy, that would be the end of the matter. *One of the most important benefits of a corporation is that it shields the shareholders and officers from personal liability for business debts.*

If you are worried about liability from your business I strongly recommend that you incorporate or consider a new business form called a "limited liability company." The limited liability company offers many of the same benefits as the corporation. It may be a good idea to talk with an attorney about which form is best for you. Many attorneys are competent to handle either business form. *Shop around and get a fair price before you hire one.*

### I own a gas station. Someone told me I have to pump gas for handicapped drivers at no extra charge. Is this the law?
### "Yes."

*Dear Mr. Alderman:*
*I own a small gas station. I sell both full-service and self-service gas. Of course, there is a substantial difference in price. The other day a person with a handicapped-person license plate drove up to the self-service pump and told me I had to fill her tank for the self-service price. I told her if she wanted full service to pull up to the full service. She said there was a law that required me to fill her tank at the self-service price. I did it this time but now I want to know, is there really such a law?*

Yes. The Texas legislature passed a law in 1989 that requires a gas station that has both self- and full-service to pump gas for a handicapped person at the self-serve price. It is important to emphasize that this law only applies when you have both self- and full-service. A station that sells only self-serve does not have to pump the gas for a handicapped person and a full-service-only station does not have to charge a different price. As you see, you did the right thing and the legal thing by pumping the gas.

### Can I tow cars parked in my spaces?
### "Not without a proper sign."

*Dear Mr. Alderman:*
*I own a small store in a strip center. The management has given each store three parking spaces that we can limit to our customers. I have put up a small sign saying that the parking is for my customers and others may be towed. So far I have not had any problems. I am wondering, however, whether I really have the right to tow them. Do I?*

Probably not. Although you have the contractual right to tow them, you have not provided the proper signs required by law. Under a new state law, parking lot owners generally may only tow cars if they have very specific signs. The law provides in part that the signs must be:

1. Conspicuously visible to and facing the driver of a vehicle that enters the lot;

2. Located on the right-hand or left-hand side of each driveway through which a vehicle can enter the lot;
3. Permanently mounted on a pole, post, wall, or barrier;
4. Installed on the lot; and
5. Installed so that the bottom edge of the sign is no lower than five feet and no higher than eight feet above ground level.

The law also provides details about the sign itself. The sign must:

1. Be made of weather-resistant material;
2. Be at least 18 inches wide and 24 inches tall;
3. Contain the international symbol for towing vehicles;
4. Contain a statement describing who may and who may not park;
5. Bear the words "Unauthorized Vehicles Will Be Towed at Owner's or Operator's Expense";
6. Contain a statement of the days and hours towing is enforced; and
7. Contain a current telephone number, including the area code, that is answered 24 hours a day to enable the owner of the towed car to locate it.

The bottom line is that it is unlawful to tow any vehicle from your lot unless you have signs as discussed above. Towing without the proper sign could result in a lawsuit.

### What is the ADA?
### "A law you should know about."

*Dear Mr. Alderman:*

*I operate a small strip center shopping area. At a recent chamber of commerce meeting a speaker told us about the ADA. He stressed the importance of this law and told us we should immediately take steps to comply with it. The only specific thing I remember him saying, however, is that we should have ramps for people in wheelchairs to get in and out. I know there must be much more to this law. Exactly what does it cover, and what do I have to do to comply?*

The ADA, or Americans With Disabilities Act, is generally referred to as the "bill of rights" for the disabled. Basically, this law prohibits discrimination against an individual with a disability and requires that public transportation and public accommodations, such as a strip shopping center, must be accessible. This is a rather complex law; however, I will try and give you a brief overview. I strongly suggest you speak with your attorney to get more details.

A person with a disability is defined by the ADA as anyone with a physical or mental handicap that is a substantial impairment of a major life activity. The law also applies to people who do not have such an impairment but are still considered impaired. For example, the law covers people who have hearing or speech impairments, or anyone who does not have the physical ability to walk or see. The law also covers a cancer patient who is cured, if that person is considered by others as still being impaired. It is estimated that more than 43 million Americans have disabilities covered by the ADA.

Under the ADA an employer with 15 or more employees may not discriminate against an otherwise qualified individual because of a disability. A qualified individual is one who with or without a reasonable accommodation is able to perform the job. For example, a person in a wheelchair who is able to perform a job would be considered qualified for the purposes of the ADA even if the employer had to build a special desk to accommodate the employee. Employment discrimination claims under the ADA should be filed with the Equal Employment Opportunity Commission.

The ADA also covers most forms of public transportation and requires that new buses, trains, or other vehicles must be made accessible. This means being equipped with lifts, ramps, and wheelchair spaces or seats. The law also prohibits discrimination based on a disability. For example, a taxi may not refuse to pick up a passenger using a wheelchair.

Finally, the ADA prohibits discrimination against persons with disabilities in their use of public accommodations such as restaurants, hotels, theaters, doctors' offices, pharmacies, grocery stores, shopping centers, museums, schools, parks, and other similar establishments. Basically, the law requires that existing barriers must be removed, provided that this can be done without much difficulty or expense, and that new construction be accessible.

# Warranties

**W**HEN you buy something, you expect to get what you pay for—this is what warranty law is all about. A warranty is any promise by a seller or manufacturer to stand behind its product. To have a warranty, there is no need to use special words such as "warranty," "guarantee," or "promise." Anything said about a product that you rely on when you purchase it is usually sufficient to give rise to a warranty that the product will do what it is supposed to do. An advertisement, the salesman's promises, even a sample of the product or a model can give rise to a warranty.

Warranty law is governed by two statutes: a state law called the **Uniform Commercial Code,** and a federal law called the **Magnuson-Moss Warranty Act.** Both of these laws protect you by making a seller or a manufacturer responsible whenever a product does not live up to your expectations. As you will see from the letters in this chapter, there are a few formalities that must be followed to establish a warranty. Often, a consumer has more than adequate warranty protection, even though nothing was ever said about a warranty.

### What is a warranty?
### "More than just a tag."

*Dear Mr. Alderman:*
*I have been shopping for a new lawn mower. I found one I liked and was waiting for it to go on sale when my neighbor told me that I shouldn't buy it because it had a bad warranty. I never really thought about warranties before—they have always been just a tag hanging on the product that I never bothered to read. Just what is a warranty? And how important is it?*

Your friend is right. One of the most important parts of any purchase is the warranty you receive. In simple terms, the warranty is the obligation, or promise, of the seller of the goods as to their quality.

163

Warranties can arise by agreement, or automatically by operation of law. For example, most products come with a written warranty, which gives you specific rights, and implied warranties, which the law imposes in most sales. *But the law allows a merchant to contractually change or disclaim his warranty liability, and most written warranties are actually taking away some of the rights you would otherwise have.*

For example, if you buy a lawn mower and nothing is said about warranties, you have an implied warranty that the mower will cut grass, and if it doesn't, the dealer is responsible. (This warranty is discussed further in the letter on pages 166–169.) But a dealer can sell a lawn mower with no warranties at all by contractually disclaiming them, for example, selling it "as is." If this was done you would have no right to return it if you got the mower home and it only ran for one hour. In fact, the dealer doesn't even promise you that it will run. When you buy without a warranty you accept all the risks that the product is defective.

In your case, consider the warranty as part of what you are buying. For instance, let's assume that a store has a lawn mower that sells for $150, but has only a limited 30-day warranty covering replacement of parts, not labor. Another store is selling a similar mower for $175, but this one has a one-year warranty that covers parts and labor. Which is the better deal? Well, the ultimate decision is up to you, but if the mower breaks down during the year, and repairs are more than $25, you would be much better off with the "more expensive" mower.

*Remember, your legal rights against a seller are based on the warranty you receive. If you have a good remedy, you will be well-protected if something goes wrong. You should shop around for warranties just like you shop for color or price.*

### What is the difference between a "full" warranty and a "limited" warranty? "Read the small print."

*Dear Mr. Alderman:*
*Whenever I shop around for a good warranty, I notice that most of them say they are a "limited" warranty. What does this mean? What is limited? If I don't want a limited warranty, what other choice do I have? Is there such a thing as an unlimited warranty?*

Recently Congress found that there were so many problems with warranty law that it passed what is called the **Magnuson-Moss Warranty**

**Act.** This law requires that warranties be written in simple and readily understandable language. It also requires that all warranties be labeled either *full* or *limited*. Under the law a warranty can only be called full if it meets these requirements:

1. The warrantor (the person making the warranty) must repair or replace the product, or give the consumer a refund within a reasonable time and at no charge, if the product does not conform with the warranty;
2. The warrantor may not impose any limitation on the duration of any implied warranty (those warranties that arise by operation of law and are discussed on pages 163 and 166);
3. The warrantor may not exclude or limit consequential damages (those caused by the defective product) unless the exclusion is conspicuously written on the face of the warranty;
4. If the product can't be repaired after a reasonable number of attempts, the consumer must be permitted to elect to receive a refund or a replacement.
5. The warranty is good for anyone who owns the product during the warranty period.

*Under the law any warranty that does not live up to all of these requirements must be labeled "limited."* When you see the word limited, the company is telling you it has not given you all the protection it could have. *A full warranty is always better than a limited one.* For example, here and on the following pages are two full warranties. Read them and see what rights you have if the product does work:

As you can see, the company tells you in simple language that if there is anything wrong with the product, you, or any other owner, can get it replaced, at no charge. In bold print, the second warranty also tells you what damages it is not responsible for: "commercial damages." The com-

**A full warranty.**

---

## MAXELL FULL LIFETIME WARRANTY

Maxell warrants this product to be free from manufacturing defects in materials and workmanship for the lifetime of the original purchaser. *This warranty does not apply to normal wear or to damage resulting from accident, abnormal use, misuse, abuse or neglect.* Any defective product will be replaced at no charge if it is returned to an authorized Maxell dealer or to Maxell. HOWEVER, MAXELL SHALL NOT BE LIABLE FOR ANY COMMERCIAL DAMAGES, WHETHER INCIDENTAL, CONSEQUENTIAL OR OTHERWISE.

panies are responsible for all other damages; for example, if the product caused damage to another piece of equipment, or if the cooler damaged your food.

On page 167 is a limited warranty. Can you see what the company has not given you? If the company can't fix the product, do you have to keep taking it back? What damages is the company liable for if the goods are defective? Who pays for labor, insurance? Can someone else use the warranty or is it limited to the original purchaser?

*The Magnuson-Moss Warranty Law applies to any consumer product costing more than $10. Under the law, warranties must be available before the sale. Take advantage of the law and read the warranty before you buy. You should shop for warranties the same way you shop for price and quality.*

### What if he didn't say anything about a warranty? Am I out of luck? "No, just the opposite."

*Dear Mr. Alderman:*
*The other day I went into the hardware store to buy a shovel to plant some bushes. The store had six or seven different models of pointed shovels, so I picked out the one that seemed the best. After coming home, I went out back to dig a hole to plant a small bush and after the first shovelful, the shovel bent. I couldn't believe it. The metal part actually bent in half. I went right back to the store and told them that I wanted my money back. They said I must have done something wrong with the shovel. They also said, "Tough luck; you bought it, it's your problem." My wife told me I should take them to small claims court, but I want to know the law first. What do you think? I am worried because I didn't get any warranty, and I always thought that when this happened it was "tough luck, buyer."*

If the store still refuses to give you your money back, take them to small claims court. The law is on your side. Under the law, whenever someone sells you something, you automatically get what is called a "warranty of merchantability." This warranty arises automatically; nothing has to be said or done. This warranty is in addition to any other warranties you may be given.

Under the warranty of merchantability, a merchant guarantees that any product he sells you is fit for its "ordinary purposes" and will "pass without objection in the trade." What this means is that whenever you buy some-

A limited warranty leaves out some protection. Read it carefully.

# COMPACT DISC PLAYER
# LIMITED WARRANTY

Toshiba America, Inc. ("TAI") and Toshiba Hawaii, Inc. ("THI") make the following limited warranties. These limited warranties extend to the original consumer purchaser or any person receiving this set as a gift from the original consumer purchaser and to no other purchaser or transferee.

### Limited One (1) Year Warranty
TAI and THI warrant this product and its parts against defects in materials or workmanship for a period of one year after the date of original retail purchase. During this period, TAI and THI will repair a defective product or part, without charge to you. You must deliver the entire product to TAI/THI Service Center. You pay for all transportation and insurance charges for the product to and from the Service Center.

### Limited One (1) Year Warranty of Parts
TAI and THI further warrant the parts in this product against defects in materials or workmanship for a period of one year after the date of original retail purchase. During this period, TAI and THI will replace a defective part without charge to you, except that if a defective part is replaced after ninety (90) days from the date of the original retail purchase you pay labor charges involved in the replacement. You must deliver the entire product to one of the TAI/THI Service Centers listed below. You pay for all transportation and insurance charges for the product to and from the Service Center.

### Owner's Manual and Warranty Registration
You should read the owner's manual thoroughly before operating this product. You should also insure that your name and address are on file as owners of a TAI/THI product by completing and mailing the attached registration card within ten days who has given you this product as a gift, purchased this product. This is one way to enable TAI/THI to establish the date of purchase of the product, as well as to provide you with better customer service and improved products. Failure to return the card will not affect your rights under this warranty so long as you retain other proof of purchase such as a bill of sale.

### Your Responsibility
The above warranties are subject to the following conditions:
(1)  You must retain your bill of sale or provide other proof of purchase. Completing and mailing in the attached registration card within ten days after the original retail purchase is one way of providing such other proof of purchase.
(2)  You must notify one of the TAI/THI Service Centers listed below within thirty (30) days after you discover a defective product or part.
(3)  All warranty servicing of this product must be make by TAI/THI Service Center.
(4)  These warranties are effective only if the product is purchased and operated in the U.S.A.
(5)  Warranties extend only to defects in materials or workmanship as limited above and do not extend to any product or parts which have been lost or discarded by you or to damage to products or parts caused by misuse, accident, improper installation, improper maintenance or repair or use in violation of instructions furnished by us; or to units which have been altered or modified without authorization of TAI/THI or to damage to products or parts thereof which have had the serial number removed, altered, defaced or rendered illegible.

### Step-By-Step Procedures—How to Obtain Warranty Service
To obtain warranty servicing, you should:
(1)  Contact one of the TAI/THI Service Centers listed below for warranty service or call the TAI toll free number 800-631-3811 within thirty (30) days after you find a defective product or part.
(2)  Arrange for the delivery of the product to the TAI/THI Service Center. Products shipped to the Service Center must be insured and safely and securely packed, preferably in the original shipping carton and a letter explaining the defect and also a copy of bill of sale or other proof of purchase must be enclosed. All transportation and insurance charges must be prepaid by you.
      (See TOSHIBA SERVICE PROCEDURE for packing suggestions)
(3)  If you have any question about service, please contact one of the following TAI/THI Service Centers:

| Toshiba America, Inc. | Toshiba America, Inc. | Toshiba America, Inc. | Toshiba Hawaii, Inc. |
|---|---|---|---|
| Service Center | Service Center | Service Center | 327 Kamakee Street |
| 82 Totowa Road | 19500 South Vermont Ave. | 2900 MacArthur Blvd. | Honolulu, Hawaii 96814 |
| Wayne, New Jersey 07470 | Torrance, Cal. 90502 | Northbrook, Ill. 60062 | Phone Number: |
| Phone Number: | Phone Number: | Phone Number: | (808) 521-5377 |
| (201) 628-8000 | (213) 538-9960 | (312) 564-1200 | |
| | (213) 770-3300 | | |

ALL WARRANTIES IMPLIED BY STATE LAW, INCLUDING THE IMPLIED WARRANTIES OF MERCHANTABILITY AND FITNESS FOR A PARTICULAR PURPOSE, ARE EXPRESSLY LIMITED TO THE DURATION OF THE LIMITED WARRANTIES SET FORTH ABOVE. Some states do not allow limitations on how long an implied warranty lasts, so the above limitation may not apply to you. WITH THE EXCEPTION OF ANY WARRANTIES IMPLIED BY STATE LAW AS HEREBY LIMITED, THE FOREGOING EXPRESS WARRANTY IS EXCLUSIVE AND IN LIEU OF ALL OTHER WARRANTIES, GUARANTEES, AGREEMENTS AND SIMILAR OBLIGATIONS OF MANUFACTURER OR SELLER WITH RESPECT TO THE REPAIR OR REPLACEMENT OF ANY PRODUCT OR PARTS.
IN NO EVENT SHALL TAI OR THI BE LIABLE FOR CONSEQUENTIAL OR INCIDENTAL DAMAGES. Some states do not allow the exclusion or limitation of incidental or consequential damages so the above limitaion may not apply to you.

No person, agent, distributor, dealer, service station or company is authorized to change, modify or extend the terms of these warranties in any manner whatsoever. The time within which an action must be commenced to enforce any obligation of TAI and THI arising under this warranty or under any statute, or law of the United States or any state thereof, is hereby limited to one year from the date you discover or should have discovered, the defect. This limitation does not apply to implied warranties arising under state law. Some states do not permit limitation of the time within which you may bring an action beyond the limits provided by state law so the above provision may not apply to you. This warranty gives you specific legal rights and you may also have other rights which vary from state to state.

**TOSHIBA AMERICA, INC.    TOSHIBA HAWAII, INC.**

*Keep this card for your record.*    Printed in Japan  22957651    **TOSHIBA**

BTV/MHF/RD/RC-80A

**Full warranties offer the most protection.**

THIS WARRANTY SUPERSEDES ALL OTHER PRODUCT WARRANTIES
INCLUDING ANY WARRANTY WHICH MAY BE FOUND IN THE USE
AND CARE BOOKLET

# FULL ONE YEAR WARRANTY

This appliance is warranted against defects in materials or workmanship for a full one year from the date of purchase.

During the warranty period this product will be repaired or replaced, at Hamilton Beach's option, at no cost to you.

In event of a [warranted] product defect, please deliver the product to the nearest authorized service station, listed on the reverse side of this warranty [or look in your local yellow pages for your nearest authorized Hamilton Beach Service Station].

This warranty does not apply in cases of abuse, mishandling, unauthorized repair or commercial use.

In using your new appliance, as directed in the Use and Care Booklet, we are confident it will serve you faithfully. Should you ever feel our products or services do not meet our high standards, please direct your comments to:

PRINTED IN U.S.A.
3-266-223-00-00

Manager, Consumer Relations
P.O. Box 2028
Washington, N. C. 27889

**Hamilton Beach Division**

Scovill

---

thing, the merchant promises you that it is going to do what you think it will do. In your case, the merchant automatically made a warranty that the shovel is fit for its ordinary purpose—that is, digging holes. When the shovel bent, the warranty was breached, and you are entitled to damages.

In other words, *when nothing is said about a warranty, the law gives you a substantial one. The law gives you a guarantee that what you bought will do what it is designed to do, the way it is supposed to do it, and for as long as a reasonable person would think it would do it.*

I suggest you go back to the store and try again to settle the problem. Let the store know that you know about warranty law. *Also remember that any breach of warranty automatically violates the Deceptive Trade Practices Act. As the next letter shows, this gives you added leverage when dealing with a merchant.*

### My laundry ruined my shirt. What can I do?
### "There is a warranty."

*Dear Mr. Alderman:*

*I recently took a new shirt to the laundry to have it cleaned. When I picked it up I noticed there were several small holes in it. I know they were not there when I took it in because it was the first time I had worn it. The laundry said, "Tough luck. Sometimes the machines do that. It is not our fault." He agreed to give me a few dollars, but the shirt cost $25. I want to take him to small claims court. Do you think I have a case?*

Whenever someone performs a service for you, there is an "implied warranty" that they will do it in a good and workmanlike manner. This means that they will maintain the same standards as others in the business and will perform as a reasonable person would expect. In my opinion, putting holes in a shirt would breach this warranty. It is not good and workmanlike cleaning to ruin the clothes.

You should also know that any time a warranty is breached this also constitutes a violation of the Deceptive Trade Practices Act. In other words, the cleaners could be responsible for as much as $75 if you took him to small claims court. Reread the material on pages 104–106 to find out how to use this law.

### What can I do if the food made me sick?
### "There may be a warranty."

*Dear Mr. Alderman:*

*The other night my friends and I went to a restaurant for dinner. After my appetizer I felt a little nauseated. By the time I got home, I was very sick. I went to the hospital, and they said it was food poisoning. I was sick for two days and spent nearly $200 on doctor bills. I went back to the restaurant, and they refused to help pay for my expenses. Do I have any legal rights?*

Under the law, whenever someone sells you food, they make what is known as a warranty of "merchantability." This, basically, is a guarantee that the food is fit for its ordinary purpose, consumption. Selling tainted food would breach this warranty and give you a claim for damages.

I should point out that this is what is known as an implied warranty, and it arises even though nothing is said about the food. Therefore, if you were to eat in a restaurant and get sick because of tainted food, the restaurant would be liable. As the next letter indicates, this could result in substantial damages.

**Is it really worth suing for breach of warranty?**
**"In Texas you get three times your damages."**

*Dear Mr. Alderman:*

*My husband and I recently bought a plant-light lamp. It came with a written guarantee that said it would be suitable for special "plant lightbulbs." When we got it home we set it up in front of our plants and put in a new bulb. After a few hours we smelled something burning and realized that the lamp casing was melting from the heat of the bulb. Luckily there wasn't a fire, but it did burn our favorite plant.*

*When we went back to the store they told us that it was the manufacturer's fault and they, the store, would not stand by the warranty. The manufacturer is in El Paso and we are in Dallas. We wrote them but they haven't responded. The light cost $69 and our plant was worth at least $20. My husband says for $89 we should just forget it; no lawyer would take it, and small claims court takes a lot of time. It seems like the person with the little claim is just out of luck. Can't something be done?*

*Ask your husband if he would go to small claims court if he would get $267 plus court costs, because under the law that is how much you will recover if you are successful.* According to Texas law, any breach of warranty automatically violates the Deceptive Trade Practices Act, and that act entitles you to three times your damages plus court costs and attorney's fees.

Based on what you say in your letter, you clearly have a claim against the manufacturer, for breach of an express warranty, and you also probably have a claim against the dealer for breach of the warranty of merchantability (re-read the letter on pages 166–169). I suggest you read Chapter Ten and find out how to use the Deceptive Trade Practices Act. My guess is once you contact the store and the manufacturer, and tell them that they may stand to lose a lot of money, they will quickly settle the matter.

*Texas warranty law is very favorable to consumers. Under the law you are always entitled to your attorney's fees plus court costs and up to three times your damages if you have to sue. Merchants know the law. Let them know you know it, too, and see how quickly problems are resolved.*

### I just bought a lemon, Can you help?
### "Texas lemon-aid."

*Dear Mr. Alderman:*
*I just bought a new car. It stinks! Ever since the day I got it, I have had nothing but problems: first the brakes, then the transmission, now the air conditioning. The car has been in the shop for over two months, and I have only owned it for three. I need help. Is there anything I can do?*

Fortunately for you, the law has changed. Until recently when you bought a car, you lived by the old maxim "caveat emptor" (let the buyer beware). Once you took the car off the lot, it was *yours,* and if it was a lemon, *you* were just out of luck. But not so today. Now, when you buy a car, the law is "caveat vendor" (let the seller beware). If you buy a lemon, the law places a burden on the seller to promptly take care of the problem, and you have strong remedies if he doesn't.

There are three separate laws a consumer can rely on after buying what turns out to be a lemon.

1. The Texas Deceptive Trade Practices Act
2. The Uniform Commercial Code
3. The Texas Lemon Law

The Texas Deceptive Trade Practices Act, discussed in Chapter Ten, simply states that if the seller deceives you as to the nature of the automobile, or if there is a breach of warranty, you may be entitled to three times your damages, plus your attorney's fees. You should read over Chapter Ten, but I want to emphasize one thing here: *If you are having a problem getting your car repaired properly, let the dealer know that you know about the Deceptive Trade Practices Act. You may be amazed at how fast the mechanics improve.*

Another law that can help you with a lemon is the **Uniform Commercial Code.** This law can be somewhat complicated, so I will just give a brief summary of what it does. If you think it applies to your problem, you will probably have to get an attorney to help you.

The Uniform Commercial Code lets a person "revoke his acceptance." In simple, nonlegal terms, this means that you can change your mind and not keep the car after you have taken it. You are allowed to "revoke your acceptance" whenever there is a defect in the car that substantially impairs its value to you, and you took the car without knowing about this defect and without having a reasonable opportunity to discover it. After you revoke your acceptance, you can give the car back to the seller, and he must give you back your money. It is as if you never took the car.

For example, if you buy a new car and, as soon as you get it home, you discover that it won't go into reverse, you can return the car and revoke your acceptance. In other words, the law gives you a chance to make sure that what you bought is what it was supposed to be. If it is not, you don't have to keep it.

If you buy a car that quickly turns out to be a lemon, you may have the right to revoke your acceptance and retrieve your money. But you must show that the defects in the car substantially impair its value to you and that you didn't know about them when you bought the car. *The application of this law can be affected by your contract with the seller. Before thinking you can revoke your acceptance and return your lemon, read your contract and see an attorney!*

The final law that may help you with your lemon is the **Texas Lemon Law.** Basically, this law applies only to new vehicles and provides that if you buy a lemon, the *manufacturer* must either return your money or give you a new car. Before you get your new auto though, two things must happen.

First:
    Your car must meet the statutory definition of a lemon.
Second:
    You must arbitrate your dispute with the Texas Motor Vehicle Commission and give the manufacturer a chance to fix things.

Under the law, a lemon is defined as a car that has a serious defect that has been reported within the warranty term and has not been repaired in a reasonable number of attempts. A dealer or manufacturer has a reasonable number of attempts to fix the car:

1. When you have taken the car to be repaired two times for the same problem within the first 12 months or 12,000 miles, whichever occurs first, and twice more during the 12 months or 12,000 miles after the second repair attempt; or
2. A serious safety defect is subject to repair once during the first 12 months or 12,000 miles, whichever occurs first, and once more during the 12 months or 12,000 miles following the first repair; or
3. The car has been out of service for a total of 30 days or more during the first 24 months or 24,000 miles, whichever occurs first, and there were two repair attempts during the first 12 months or 12,000 miles, and a substantial problem still exists. Any time for which you were provided a free loaner car does not count toward the 30 days.

In other words, if your car has a defect that substantially affects the use or value of the car, and that defect is not repaired within the above time limits, it meets the definition of a legal "lemon."

To make certain you protect yourself under the lemon law, or for that matter, any time you have a lemon, be sure that the dealer documents your problem each time you bring your car in. Also, tell him your problem in general terms. Under the law you must have had the car in four times for the same defect. If your engine stalls out, just tell them that, and make sure that is how it is written up on the service order. If you complain about the carburetor and then bring it back saying it is the fuel pump, and then the fuel line, you will have three different problems, not one problem repaired three times. *It is the dealer's job to pinpoint the exact nature of your problem. Describe the problem in general, nonmechanical terms and let the dealer worry about the exact nature of the defect.*

Once you think you have met the test for a lemon, you must contact the Motor Vehicle Commission and ask to arbitrate the dispute with the manufacturer. The commission will listen to your complaint and has the power to order the manufacturer to refund your money—or give you a new car.

You can write the motor vehicle commission at: Texas Motor Vehicle Commission, P.O. Box 2293, Austin, TX 78768, or call them at (512) 476-3618 or (800) 622-8682.

# CHAPTER EIGHTEEN

# Wills & Probate

ONE of the most common questions asked is: "Do I need a will?" Well, frankly, no; you don't need a will. It really isn't going to matter to you. But on the other hand, it may be extremely important to your family, because the only way you can ensure they receive your property, with a minimum of time and expense, is to make out a will.

When you die without a will, you are said to have died "intestate." If you die intestate, the state decides who gets your property. The process of distributing your property and seeing that all of your bills are paid is usually closely supervised by the court.

But, if you die with a will, you can give your property to whomever you wish, and you can also appoint an "executor" to handle the distribution of the property. Usually the executor can act without the supervision of the court. In other words, *having a will is the most effective way to make certain your property goes where you want—and that your estate is not tied-up with the additional time and expense of court supervision.*

### What is a "living will"?
### "Death with dignity."

*Dear Mr. Alderman:*
*A friend told me that a law exists in Texas that permits a person to refuse to be kept alive by machines—when he is going to die anyway. Should I ever be diagnosed as terminal, I would not wish my family to pay for expensive treatment simply to allow me to live a little longer. What can I do to make certain I can refuse such treatment? What if I am in a coma? How, then, can I protect my family?*

There is a legal device designed to let you make the choice of whether to be left on a life-sustaining machine after you have been found to be terminally ill. The document is called *a directive to physicians.* The common name given to this document is "living will."

Generally, if you are being kept alive by a machine, a physician will not disconnect you or turn the machine off without your consent even if your family requests it. This is because of the potential liability to the doctor. Recently, however, the Texas legislature passed a law that lets you decide in advance whether to be kept alive by a machine. If you execute a directive under this law, the physician can follow your wishes without worrying about liability to your estate or your heirs. Although a doctor is not obligated to comply with a living will, most do.

Under the Texas Natural Death Act, you can fill out a written directive at any time, or, you may make an oral directive in front of two witnesses and your doctor. Because you may not be competent to make such a decision when you need to, it is a good idea to make out a directive now and keep it in a safe place.

A natural death act directive, or living will, does not have to be in any special form, but the form on pages 205–206 is suggested by the legislature. Even though it is not necessary in Texas to have a directive notarized, you may want to do so just in case you are in a state that requires it.

*The directive to physicians gives you the choice to die with dignity, and avoid costly medical bills for your family. The choice is up to you. If you want to make that choice, simply fill in the form, have it notarized, and keep it in a safe place where your family can find it.*

For more free information about your right to die a natural death, write: The Society for the Right to Die, 250 W. 57th St., New York, NY 10107.

**I am going into the hospital for very complicated surgery.
Is there some way my son can make medical decisions for me
if I am not competent to do so?
"Yes, through a Durable Power of Attorney for Health Care."**

*Dear Mr. Alderman:*
*I am 72 years old and just found out that I have a tumor that must be removed. The doctors said that it is a very serious operation and that I may not recover.*
*I am able to face the possibility of death but I am concerned about being subjected to unwanted medical treatment. For example, I do not want to be kept alive by a feeding tube when all hope for recovery is gone. I know that a living will gives me the right to have life support systems disconnected if I have a terminal condition but I would like to have some control over the type and extent of treatment*

*I receive. I trust my son's judgment and want to know if there is some way to have him make my medical decisions in the event I cannot.*

Texas has passed a law that lets you have your wish. The Durable Power of Attorney for Health Care law allows a person to appoint another to make health care decisions for him. First, you must be given a copy of the Durable Power of Attorney Disclosure form. Then, if you complete the proper form, your son could be appointed to make your health care decisions in the event you were not competent to do so. This would give him the right to refuse treatment for you. As long as you trust that your son will execute the judgment you want, this form is the way to ensure that he has that right. I should also point out that you can revoke the power of attorney by just telling your doctor.

### If there a difference between a durable power of attorney and a durable power of attorney for health care?
### "Yes, a big difference."

*Dear Mr. Alderman:*
*I am seriously ill and do not think I will be able to manage my affairs for much longer. I want to give my son the authority to make medical decisions for me and to pay all my bills and handle my financial affairs. I filled out a durable power of attorney for health care last year. Now I have been told there is another type of power of attorney I must complete. What is it?*

As you already know, a durable power of attorney for health care allows you to designate someone else to make medical decisions regarding your health care, in the event that you are unable to. This document does not, however, grant any other authority.

If you want to authorize someone else to make your financial decisions, you must fill out a Durable Power of Attorney. This document is a very powerful, legally binding form that gives someone else the power to make decisions regarding your property and financial matters in the event you become disabled or otherwise incapable of making decisions. For example, the person designated as your agent may write checks on your account to pay your bills and can withdraw money from any of your accounts as needed. This power, however, is very broad. Money can be withdrawn to pay your bills, or it could just be taken and used for a trip to Hawaii.

*(text continued on page 181)*

**Durable Power of Attorney for Health Care form.**

## DURABLE POWER OF ATTORNEY FOR HEALTH CARE DESIGNATION OF HEALTH CARE AGENT.

I, _____ (insert your name) appoint:

Name:_____

Address:_____ Phone _____

as my agent to make any and all health care decisions for me, except to the extent I state otherwise in this document. This durable power of attorney for health care takes effect if I become unable to make my own health care decisions and this fact is certified in writing by my physician.

LIMITATIONS ON THE DECISION MAKING AUTHORITY OF MY AGENT ARE AS FOLLOWS:_____

### DESIGNATION OF ALTERNATE AGENT.

(You are not required to designate an alternate agent but you may do so. An alternate agent may make the same health care decisions as the designated agent if the designated agent is unable or unwilling to act as your agent. If the agent designated is your spouse, the designation is automatically revoked by law if your marriage is dissolved.)

If the person designated as my agent is unable or unwilling to make health care decisions for me, I designate the following persons to serve as my agent to make health care decisions for me as authorized by this document, who serve in the following order:

A. First Alternate Agent
    Name:_____
    Address:_____ Phone _____
B. Second Alternate Agent
    Name:_____
    Address:_____ Phone _____

The original of this document is kept at _____
The following individuals or institutions have signed copies:
    Name:_____
    Address:_____
    Name:_____
    Address:_____

## DURATION.

I understand that this power of attorney exists indefinitely from the date I execute this document unless I establish a shorter time or revoke the power of attorney. If I am unable to make health care decisions for myself when this power of attorney expires, the authority I have granted my agent continues to exist until the time I become able to make health care decisions for myself.

(IF APPLICABLE) This power of attorney ends on _____

## PRIOR DESIGNATIONS REVOKED.

I revoke any prior durable power of attorney for health care.

## ACKNOWLEDGEMENT OF DISCLOSURE STATEMENT.

I have been provided with a disclosure statement explaining the effect of this document. I have read and understand the information contained in the disclosure statement.

(YOU MUST DATE AND SIGN THIS POWER OF ATTORNEY)

I sign my name to this durable power of attorney for health care on

_____ 19 ___,   _____
                                   (City and State)

_____          _____
      (Signature)                  (Print Name)

## STATEMENT OF WITNESSES.

I declare under penalty of perjury that the principal has identified himself or herself to me, that the principal signed or acknowledged this durable power of attorney in my presence, that I believe the principal to be of sound mind, that the principal has affirmed that the principal is aware of the nature of the document and is signing it voluntarily and free from duress, that the principal requested that I serve as witness to the principal's execution of this document, that I am not the person appointed as agent by this document, and that I am not a provider of health or residential care, an employee of a provider of health or residential care, the operator of a community care facility, or an employee of an operator of a health care facility.

I declare that I am not related to the principal by blood, marriage, or adoption and that to the best of my knowledge I am not entitled to any part of the estate of the principal on the death of the principal under a will or by operation of law.

Witness Signature:_____ Print Name: _____

Address:_____ Date: _____

Witness Signature:_____ Print Name: _____

Address:_____ Date: _____

**Disclosure Statement form
for Durable Power of Attorney for Health Care.**

## INFORMATION CONCERNING THE DURABLE POWER OF ATTORNEY FOR HEALTH CARE

THIS IS AN IMPORTANT LEGAL DOCUMENT. BEFORE SIGNING THIS DOCUMENT, YOU SHOULD KNOW THESE IMPORTANT FACTS:

Except to the extent you state otherwise, this document gives the person you name as your agent the authority to make any and all health care decisions for you in accordance with your wishes, including your religious and moral beliefs, when you are no longer capable of making them yourself. Because "health care" means any treatment, service, or procedure to maintain, diagnose, or treat your physical or mental condition, your agent has the power to make a broad range of health care decisions for you. Your agent may consent, refuse to consent, or withdraw consent to medical treatment and may make decisions about withdrawing or withholding life-sustaining treatment. Your agent may not consent to voluntary inpatient mental health services, convulsive treatment, psychosurgery, or abortion. A physician must comply with your agent's instructions or allow you to be transferred to another physician.

Your agent's authority begins when your doctor certifies that you lack the capacity to make health care decisions.

Your agent is obligated to follow your instructions when making decisions on your behalf. Unless you state otherwise, your agent has the same authority to make decisions about your health care as you would have had.

It is important that you discuss this document with your physician or other health care provider before you sign it to make sure that you understand the nature and range of decisions that may be made on your behalf. If you do not have a physician, you should talk with someone else who is knowledgeable about these issues and can answer your questions. You do not need a lawyer's assistance to complete this document, but if there is anything in this document that you do not understand, you should ask a lawyer to explain it to you.

The person you appoint as agent should be someone you know and trust. The person must be 18 years of age or older or a person under 18 years of age who has had the disabilities of minority removed. If you appoint your health or residential care provider (e.g., your physician or an employee of a home health agency, hospital, nursing home, or residential care home, other than a relative), that person has to choose between acting as your agent or as your health or residential care provider; the law does not permit a person to do both at the same time.

You should inform the person you appoint that you want the person to be your health care agent. You should discuss this document with your agent and your physician and give each a signed copy. You should indicate on the document itself the people and institutions who have signed copies. Your agent is not liable for health care decisions made in good faith on your behalf.

Even after you have signed this document, you have the right to make health care decisions for yourself as long as you are able to do so and treatment cannot be given to you or stopped over your objection. You have the right to revoke the authority granted to your agent by informing your agent of your health or residential care provider orally or in writing, or by your execution of a subsequent durable power of attorney for health care. Unless you state otherwise, your appointment of a spouse dissolves on divorce.

This document may not be changed or modified. If you want to make changes in the document, you must make an entirely new one.

You may wish to designate an alternate agent in the event that your agent is unwilling, unable, or ineligible to act as your agent. Any alternate agent you designate has the same authority to make health care decisions for you. THIS POWER OF ATTORNEY IS NOT VALID UNLESS IT IS SIGNED IN THE PRESENCE OF TWO OR MORE QUALIFIED WITNESSES. THE FOLLOWING PERSONS MAY NOT ACT AS WITNESSES:

(1) the person you have designated as your agent;
(2) your health or residential care provider or an employee of your health or residential care provider;
(3) your spouse;
(4) your lawful heirs or beneficiaries named in your will or a deed; or
(5) creditors or persons who have a claim against you.

*(text continued from page 176)*

Before you sign a durable power of attorney and designate someone as your agent, you must give very serious consideration to what you are doing. You also may want to contact an attorney to make sure you grant only as much power as you have to.

I have attached a Statutory Durable Power of Attorney form on pages 207 to 209. This is the form suggested by the legislature. Any document in substantially the same form is effective. As you can tell, the law lets you determine the extent of the powers you grant to your agent. Once you sign the document, however, anyone who in good faith relies on it is protected, even if your agent doesn't do what you wanted.

### What is "community property"?
### "Half yours . . . half your spouse's."

*Dear Mr. Alderman:*
*Recently I have married and my friends tell me that, henceforth, all my property is considered "community property" and that I should keep track of the property I owned prior to the marriage. What does it matter?*

When people get married, all of their property is either "community" or separate. This distinction is important because it determines who gets what upon death or divorce. Basically, community property is everything that people acquire after they get married. Separate property is everything you owned before you were married, and gifts or inheritances acquired after you are married. *Community property is considered to be owned one-half by each spouse. Separate property belongs solely to the spouse who owned or acquired it.* Why is this important? Because when the marriage ends, either by death or divorce, community property is split between the parties or the heirs, while separate property goes to just one spouse or his or her heirs. Let me give you an example.

Suppose you are about to get married. You own a car, some clothes, furniture and you have about $5,000 in the bank. Your wife-to-be has about the same property. You marry, and both open bank accounts in your own names. After a few years you buy a house with money you saved after you were married, and you also buy a car. During the marriage your rich aunt dies and leaves you $25,000. If, at this point, one of you should die, or if you divorce, the house and car would be community property. This means that if you were to divorce you would split them (or the money obtained from their sale), and if one of you died, his heirs would acquire a one-half interest in the house and car. On the other hand, the money you put in the bank saved from your pre-marriage earnings and the money received from your aunt are separate property. This means that upon divorce it would be exclusively yours, and if you died all of it would go to your heirs. You should be aware, though, that the interest earned on your separate property is community property, and your spouse is entitled to one-half of that amount.

*In Texas, people do not pay alimony upon divorce. Property is split according to community property laws, and that is the end of it. Remember, once you get married nearly everything you acquire will be considered community property and will be owned equally by both spouses.*

If you are concerned about the community property law—for example, you are an older person getting married for a second time and you want to make sure your first family is taken care of—you can enter into a contract to change the community property laws. Recently Texas amended its laws to allow people to decide how their property will be designated. If you think this is something you may be interested in, you should consult an attorney.

### What if I don't have a will?
### "The state writes one for you."

*Dear Mr. Alderman:*
*I recently remarried. My wife and I both have children from our prior marriages and now want to have children together. My friends have told me that it is important to have a will if I want to ensure that the children of my first marriage are taken care of. I am going to have a will prepared, but I am curious: what happens if I die without a will?*

If you die without a will, the state, in effect, writes one for you. There are very specific laws that determine to whom your property passes after your death. This determination is based on the type of property, whether it is separate or community, and who survives you—for example, is your spouse living, are your children living? If you are interested in a general idea of what happens in a specific case, you should first read the previous letter to find out what property is separate and what property is community, and then look at the charts on pages 183–185. As you can see, the process can get very complicated, and the best advice I can give you is to prepare a will. *Remember: If you have a will, your property is divided as you direct.*

If you want your property to go to someone other than the person(s) it would go to according to the charts, you must have a will. A good example of how complicated it can get without a will is what could happen in your case (see page 184). If you died without a will, the house that you bought with your second wife would go half to your second wife and half to the children of your first marriage. This probably is not what you would choose to do in a will. *You always have a choice of where your property goes after your death—simply write a will.*

---

### Married Man or Woman With No Child or Children (Father and Mother Surviving)

**A. SEPARATE PROPERTY**

Real Estate

All Other Property

If only one parent survives, he or she takes ¼ of the real estate in the separate property and ¼ is equally divided between brothers and sisters of the deceased, and their decendants. If there are no surviving brothers and sisters, then surviving parent takes ½ of real estate. If neither parent survives, then ½ of real estate is equally taken by brothers and sisters of the deceased and their descendants. If no parents, no brothers or sisters, or their descendants survive the deceased—then all the real estate is taken by the surviving husband or wife.

**B. COMMUNITY PROPERTY**

All community property—real or personal—is taken by surviving husband or wife.

---

# Married Man or Woman With Child or Children

## A. SEPARATE PROPERTY

### Real Estate

### All Other Property

Surviving husband or wife only inherits an estate for life in one-third of the land of the deceased. When such surviving husband or wife dies, all of the real estate is owned by the deceased's child or children.

## B. COMMUNITY PROPERTY

### Real Estate

*IF* all surviving children are also children of the surviving spouse.

### All Other Property

*IF* a surviving child is not also a child of the surviving spouse. Children of deceased children take their parent's share

## Unmarried Man or Woman
## or Widower or Widow
## With No Child or Children

(FATHER AND MOTHER
SURVIVING)

(FATHER OR MOTHER &
BROTHERS OR SISTERS
SURVIVING)

### Entire Estate

### Entire Estate

If only father or mother survives, then that parent takes ½, and other ½ goes equally to all brothers and sisters. If no surviving brothers or sisters or their descendants, then all estate goes to such surviving father or mother.

## Widower or Widow With
## Child or Children

### Real Estate

### All Other Property

Children of deceased children take their parent's share.

### Can I write my own will?
### "Sure, but you may not want to."

*Dear Mr. Alderman:*
*I have read a lot recently about how important it is to have a will. I have decided that I should have one and I would like to write it myself. Is this legal? How should I do it?*

It is perfectly legal for anyone to write his own will. If the will meets the requirements of the law, it will be just as valid as a will prepared by an attorney. But if you are going to write your own will, you must be careful. One small mistake can invalidate the entire will and cause real problems for your family. *For this reason, I strongly urge you to see a lawyer.*

There are two basic kinds of wills in Texas: a *holographic will,* which is one written entirely in your own handwriting and signed; and a *formal will,* which can be handwritten, printed, or typed, and which must be signed and witnessed by two people.

If you write a holographic will, it is valid so long as it is completely handwritten and signed. It is not a valid holographic will if you type part of it, or if you fill in blanks on a form. It also should be dated and it should state that it replaces all other wills you may have written. A holographic will must clearly indicate it was intended as a will and should not have any printing, typing, or obliterations. For example, the document on page 187 would serve as a holographic will.

*Holographic wills should be used only in emergency situations. Best advice: Don't rely on a holographic will. It must be letter-perfect, and it is too easy to make a mistake. If you feel you must write your own will, consider a formal will.*

A formal will must be signed by the testator and witnessed by at least two witnesses. It can be written, typed, or be part of a pre-printed form. For example, you can buy a form and fill in the proper blanks, or you could type it. You should also date your will, publish it (that is, declare it to be your will), and make sure everyone signs in the presence of everyone else. To give yourself added protection in other states, you should have three witnesses.

In addition to the proper signature, you should have what is known as a "self-proving affidavit." This allows your survivors to probate the will without having to go out and find the witnesses. A self-proving affidavit is

**A holographic will should be letter-perfect.**

> *Last Will & Testament*
>
> I, Jane Smith, a resident of Harris County, Texas, declare this to be my Last Will & Testament. I revoke all prior wills and codicils.
>
> First: I leave my 1990 Buick to my only brother, Jack Smith.
>
> Second: I leave my dog, Shasta, to Nancy Jones, who resides at 1324 West Oaks, Houston, Texas.
>
> Third: I leave the remainder of my estate to my parents, Susan Smith and Joe Smith, in equal shares. If they are not living, I leave the remainder of my property to the Society for the Prevention of Cruelty to Animals, Houston, Texas.
>
> Fourth: I nominate Larry James as independent executor of my will. If he is not living or does not want to be executor, I nominate Keith Long to act in his place. I direct that no bond be required of my executor.
>
> Executed at Houston, Texas, on July 2, 1994.
>
> *Jane Smith*

simply a notary's statement that he has seen the people sign. At the end of this chapter I have included some model wills and a self-proving affidavit.

*Although the law allows you to prepare your own will, I don't recommend it. One small mistake can totally invalidate the entire will.* To be safe, you should have an attorney prepare your will, and you should not have to pay very much money to have it done. For example, recently I telephoned 40 attorneys in Houston and asked how much they would charge to prepare a simple will for a single person. The prices ranged from $35 to over $600. I sent someone down to buy the $35 will and then had an expert look at it. It was a fine will and completely served the purposes of the person who bought it. *In other words, shop around. Most attorneys are competent to draft a simple will and you may save yourself hundreds of dollars by making a few phone calls.*

### What is an executor?
### "The person in charge."

*Dear Mr. Alderman:*
*My sister just passed away and I was told I am the executor of her will. What does this mean? Does this mean that I won't inherit anything? Will it cost me any money? I don't want to sound cheap, but I am not a wealthy man.*

When you die it is necessary for someone to gather up all of your property, close your bank accounts, transfer title to your house, and then make sure that everything is given to the people you designated in your will. This person is called an executor, if it is a man, and an executrix, if it is a woman. Usually you appoint someone you trust, who you believe is competent to do what must be done as executor or executrix. By appointing you as executor, your sister was saying that she believed you would be the best person to make sure her wishes are fulfilled.

*There is no reason why the executor or executrix cannot also receive property under a will, and if the will provides, he or she does not have to post a bond, or pay any money, to serve.*

But, in order to put the will into effect, it has to be probated. Probate is a legal proceeding that gives the executor the power to act. To probate the will you probably need an attorney. But probate is usually a routine matter and you should shop around for an attorney. Be sure to compare prices and ask how the fee is computed. Some lawyers charge a percentage while others charge by the hour. You usually will be better off paying by the hour. I should also point out that the attorney's fees are paid by the estate, not you, so you don't have to worry about this cost.

### How can I avoid probating a will?
### "You can't."

*Dear Mr. Alderman:*
*I am getting up in years, and I want to leave my children property in*
*my will without them having to go through probate. I don't have much*
*property, and it seems a waste to spend a lot of money on probate*
*costs. How can I make sure my will doesn't have to be probated?*

You can't. As I said in the previous letter, probate is the legal term
used to describe the process by which the terms of a will are given legal
effect. Any property left to someone through a will has to go through
some form of probate. Probate does not, however, have to be a long,
expensive process. In fact, there is a new form of probate called "informal probate" that is designed for small estates. Informal probate should
be very inexpensive.

If you wish to avoid any form of probate, you must either give the
property outright, as a gift, or place it in trust before you die. You may
want to speak with an attorney to find out what would be best for you in
light of your concerns about probate and tax law. There are many forms
of trusts, and before giving any gift you must consider the consequences
of the gift tax law.

### Who can be an executor?
### "Nearly anyone."

*Dear Mr. Alderman:*
*I am making out a will. A friend told me that I couldn't make my son*
*the executor of the will because he was going to inherit my property.*
*I don't know who else to use. Can I name a bank?*

The simple answer is to name your son. A person can be an executor
of a will even if he is going to inherit under the will. The only people
who may not serve as executors of a will include minors, incompetents,
convicted felons, and others the court finds unsuitable. There are also
some restrictions on when a nonresident or a corporation may act as an
executor. A nonresident may only serve if he appoints a resident agent to
accept service of process. A corporation may only serve if it is authorized to act as a fiduciary in this state.

The bottom line is that in most cases the executor is also a family
member who will inherit some property under the will. Tell your friend
he was misinformed.

## Do I have to pay estate taxes?
## "Only if you are rich."

*Dear Mr. Alderman:*
*I am 83 and I have been told that I should begin to give some of my property away to avoid paying estate taxes. I am married and we don't have much money. We own a house worth about $75,000 and maybe another $50,000 in other property. In my will I leave everything to my wife, and if she dies before me, to our children. Will my heirs have to pay very much in estate taxes?*

First, I must make one thing clear. Estate taxes, which are collected by both the state and federal governments, are not paid by your heirs. They are paid out of your estate. In other words, the money is taken before your estate is distributed to your heirs. But more importantly for you, under the present law your estate does not have to pay these taxes unless it is valued at more than $600,000. *In your case there would not be any liability for estate taxes.*

You also should know that no matter how large your estate is, no taxes have to be paid if the property goes to your spouse. For example, suppose your estate was worth $700,000; estate taxes would be due at your death. But if you left everything to your wife, no taxes would be paid. Of course, when she died, and left everything to your children, the taxes *would* have to be paid.

*If you think that your estate is going to have to pay estate taxes, you should see an attorney about doing what is called "estate planning." There are many things you can do to legally avoid paying estate taxes.*

## What is a "life estate"?
## "Another type of ownership."

*Dear Mr. Alderman:*
*Recently my father died. The lawyer in charge of things told me that my father left me his house, but that he left a "life estate" to my step-mother, so I can't have it until she dies. I don't understand. If it is my house, why do I have to let her live there? I live in a small house and it would be really nice to have a big place to live in. I don't want to sound cold, but my father had only been married to my stepmother for less than a year, and it doesn't seem fair. Is there anything I can do?*

The answer is no. What the lawyer told you is right. If your stepmother has a "life estate" in the house, it is hers, to do with as she pleases, until she dies. It then becomes yours.

When you transfer property, there are many different ways of doing it. For example, you can give it outright, as in the case of a gift or the standard provision in a will. But this is not the only way to transfer property. *When you transfer property, you do not have to make an absolute transfer. The law allows you to transfer less than an unlimited full interest.* A common example would be when you rent an apartment. The landlord has transferred an interest in the property to you, but as a lessee your interest is limited by the terms of the lease. A "life estate" is another way to transfer property. When you get a life estate you get full rights in the property, but only for as long as you live. When you die the property automatically goes to someone else.

So what rights does your stepmother have? Basically, she can do whatever she wants with the property—as if she owned it. But when she dies, it is yours. For instance, let's say she sold the property. All she has legal power to sell is her life estate, and therefore, when she died, whoever bought the property would no longer have title to it. It would be yours. The purchaser only has the same rights as your stepmother.

*A life estate is a useful way of providing for one person during his or her lifetime, while making sure that ultimate title goes to someone else.* Your father probably wanted to make sure your stepmother was comfortable for the rest of her life, but that you ultimately got the house. That is exactly the result that will occur through the use of a life estate.

### I just moved to Texas. Is my will still good? "Maybe not."

*Dear Mr. Alderman:*

*My wife and I have lived in Arkansas for over 20 years. We just moved to Texas to be near our grandchildren. We both have wills written by an Arkansas lawyer. Are they any good in Texas? We really would rather not have to spend the money to have a new will written.*

The simple answer is "I don't know." To give you an answer I would have to be an expert on Arkansas law.

Even though this is the United States of America, every state has its own laws, and is free to regulate its citizens as it sees fit. For example, in some states you can drink at 18 while in others, it's 21; although you can gamble in Nevada and Atlantic City, New Jersey, gambling is illegal in most states.

The same thing is true with respect to wills. Every state has its own requirements for what must be included in a will and what happens if you don't have one, or if you have one that is not valid. Although in most cases the requirements are the same, there is no guarantee that a will valid in one state is valid in another. *A will made up in another state is valid in Texas if it meets the requirements of Texas law.* The will is not valid, regardless of whether it is valid in the other state, if it does not comply with Texas law.

For example, Texas law requires that a will be witnessed by two people. If a will was made up in a state that required only one witness, and you had only one witness, it would not be valid when you moved to Texas. But if you make out a will in a state that requires three witnesses, it will satisfy Texas law as well. In other words, the only way to tell if the will is valid, is to examine it to see if it complies with Texas law. Because I am not an expert on Arkansas law I could not tell you if your Arkansas will is valid.

*The best advice I can give you is to take your will to an attorney and let him or her look at it to see if it complies with Texas law. You also must make sure the will does what you want with your estate.* As I said in the introduction to this section, you should shop around for an attorney before you see one. Wills are considered routine legal matters and most attorneys are competent to handle them. You may save a lot of money with a few phone calls.

### What happens to lottery winnings after I die?
### "They go to your heirs."

*Dear Mr. Alderman:*
*I have heard different reports about what happens to my lottery winnings if I die before they are paid out. Do my heirs collect the money, or does the state just get to keep the unpaid installments?*

Every state that has a lottery handles this problem in its own way. In some states, the money is paid only as long as the winner is alive. In others, including Texas, the money is considered an asset that will pass to your heirs as any other asset would.

State law dictates who your estate, including lottery winnings, goes to after your death. If you want to insure that your lottery winnings go to the person you want, with the least time and expense, make sure you have a will.

## Model Wills

As I said before, there is no one will that is right for everyone. You must consider who you want your property to go to after your death, and how you want that property to be transferred. For example, you may want property given to minors to be put in a trust until they reach a certain age.

The models that follow are just three examples of a will. One is for a single person, one is for a married person without children, and the last one is for a married person with children. Read them carefully. If the model form does what you want to do with your property, then you should consider using it. You also can make changes to fit your needs. But I still urge you to contact a lawyer to draw up a will tailored to your special needs. These forms should be thought of as merely an emergency measure until you have a chance to see a lawyer.

## Instructions:

A "testator" is a man who makes out a will and a "testatrix" is a woman. If you use these model wills, make sure you use the proper designation. Also, "executor" is used for a man and "executrix" for a woman. Be sure to read the will carefully, and when you write yours *make sure you sign each page at the bottom and at the end of the will.* You should sign in the presence of three witnesses and a notary, and you should declare it to be your will before you sign. You also should have all the witnesses sign in the presence of each other and the notary. *Be sure to attach and complete the self-proving affidavit.*

Model will for single person.

---

# LAST WILL AND TESTAMENT
## OF
## JANET GRANT

THE STATE OF TEXAS)
) KNOW ALL MEN
COUNTY OF HARRIS ) BY THESE PRESENTS

THAT, I, JANET GRANT, a resident of HARRIS County, Texas, being of sound mind and disposing memory and more than eighteen years of age, do hereby make, publish and declare this to be my Last Will and Testament, hereby revoking all Wills and Codicils heretofore made by me.

## ARTICLE I.
### Declarations

*Section 1.1* I declare that I am not now married.

*Section 1.2* No children have ever been born to or adopted by me.

*Section 1.3* It is my intention to dispose of all real and personal property which I have the right to dispose of by will.

## ARTICLE II.
### Executorship

*Section 2.1* I appoint my father, FRED GRANT of HOUSTON, Texas, Independent Executor of this my Last Will and Testament and of my Estate. Should FRED GRANT, for any reason or at any time be unable or unwilling to qualify, or for any reason fail to qualify, or, after qualifying, for any reason fail to continue to act, I designate my friend TOM POST of HOUSTON, Texas, as successor or substitute Independent Executor under this will.

As used herein the term "Executor" shall mean the person then acting under either of the foregoing appointments.

*Section 2.2* I direct that no bond or other security shall be required of my Executor and any Executor hereunder shall be independent of the supervision and direction of the Probate Court to the

_____
TESTATRIX

fullest extent permitted by law. I further direct that no action shall be had in any court of probate jurisdiction in connection with this Will or in the administration or settlement of my Estate other than the probating of this Will and the return of any inventory, appraisement and list of claims due by or owing to my Estate.

*Section 2.3* My Executor shall have, and may exercise without first obtaining the approval of any court, all of the powers of Independent Executors under the laws of the State of Texas.

## ARTICLE III.
### Bequests and Devises

*Section 3.1* I give my diamond stick pin to my sister **SUSAN GRANT,** if she survives me by 30 days; if she does not, the gift shall lapse and become part of my estate.

*Section 3.2* I hereby give, devise and bequeath the remainder of my estate, whether real, personal or mixed, and wherever situated to my parents, **FRED GRANT** and **MARTHA GRANT,** of **HOUSTON,** Texas, to share and share alike.

*Section 3.3* In the event that either **FRED GRANT** or **MARTHA GRANT** does not survive me, I give, devise, and bequeath the remainder of my property of every kind, character and description, wherever situated, whether the same is real, personal or mixed, to the survivor.

*Section 3.4* In the event that **FRED GRANT** and **MARTHA GRANT,** do not survive me, I give, devise and bequeath the remainder of my property to **TOM POST** of **HOUSTON,** Texas.

*Section 3.5* In the event that none of the persons designated herein survive me, then I direct that my estate pass to my heirs at law.

*Section 3.6* No one shall be deemed to have survived me unless that person survives at least 30 days after the date of my death.

IN WITNESS WHEREOF, I, **JANET GRANT,** testatrix, do hereby subscribe my name this the ____ day of _____, 19___, to this instrument and declare the same to be my Last Will and Testament, in the presence of _____ ,

_____

and _____

_____
TESTATRIX

attesting witnesses at my request and in my presence and in the presence of each other.

The foregoing instrument was now here published as the Last Will and Testament of JANET GRANT, and signed and subscribed by her, the Testatrix, in our presence, and we, at her request and in her presence and in the presence of each other signed and subscribed our names hereto as attesting witnesses.

Address:

_____         _____
                                         Witness

Address: _____

_____         _____
                                         Witness

Address: _____

_____         _____
                                         Witness

_____

## (ADD SELF-PROVING AFFIDAVIT)

Model will for married person with no children.

LAST WILL AND TESTAMENT
OF
CATHY NAN SIMES

STATE OF TEXAS
COUNTY OF TRAVIS
KNOW ALL MEN BY THESE PRESENTS:

THAT I, CATHY NAN SIMES, of TRAVIS County, Texas, and being of sound mind and disposing memory and above the age of eighteen (18) years, do make, publish and declare this my Last Will and Testament, hereby revoking all other wills and codicils heretofore made by me.

I.

I declare that I am married to THOMAS SIMES and that all references in this Will to my spouse are references to him. I have no child or children, living or dead, born to me or adopted, at the date of the execution of this Will.

II.

I hereby nominate and appoint my spouse, THOMAS SIMES, as Independent Executor of the Will, and I direct that no bond shall be required of him. If my spouse, THOMAS SIMES, should pre-decease me, or for any reason fail to qualify or decline to act as executor, then I nominate and appoint JOHN TAPER, of AUSTIN, TEXAS, as Independent Executor of this Will, to serve without bond or compensation. If my spouse and JOHN TAPER both fail to qualify or decline to act as executor, I nominate and appoint ALICE BRADLEY of AUSTIN, TEXAS, as Independent Executrix of this Will, to serve without bond or compensation.

My executor/executrix shall have and possess all of the rights and powers and be subject to all of the duties and responsibilities conferred and imposed on an independent executor by the Texas Probate Code as the Code now provides or as it may be hereafter amended.

I direct that no action shall be taken in any court in relation to the settlement of my estate other than the probating and recording of the Will and the return of a statutory inventory and appraisement and list of claims of my estate.

_____
TESTATRIX

### III.

I give, devise, and bequeath to my beloved spouse, **THOMAS SIMES,** all of my property, real, personal, and mixed, and where-soever located, of every sort and description of which I may die possessed, or to which I may be entitled at the time of my death, to have and to hold as his property absolutely.

### IV.

If my spouse, **THOMAS SIMES,** should predecease me, or if he and I die as a result of a common disaster or under such circumstances that there is not sufficient evidence to determine the order of our deaths, or if my spouse, **THOMAS SIMES,** shall die within a period of 30 days after the date of my death, then all bequests, devises and provisions made herein to or for his benefit shall be void and my estate shall be administered and distributed in all respects as though my spouse, **THOMAS SIMES,** had not survived me.

### V.

If my spouse, **THOMAS SIMES,** does not survive me, I give the sum of ten thousand dollars ($10,000) to **SANDY WRIGHT** of **HOUSTON, TEXAS,** if she survives me, and I give, devise, and bequeath my Hammond organ, automobile, jewelry and the residue of my estate to **JOHN TAPER** of **AUSTIN, TEXAS,** if he survives me.

### VI.

In the event that **JOHN TAPER,** does not survive me, then I direct that my estate pass to my heirs at law.

### VII.

No one shall be deemed to have survived me unless that person survives at least 30 days after the date of my death.

### VIII.

If any beneficiary under this will in any manner, directly or indirectly, contests or attacks this will or any of its provisions, any share or interest in my estate given to the contesting beneficiary under this will is revoked and shall be disposed of in the same manner provided herein as if that contesting beneficiary had predeceased me without issue.

———————————————
**TESTATRIX**

## IX.

I declare that I have made and paid for funeral arrangements with **PLEASANT VALLEY REST, AUSTIN, TEXAS,** and I direct my executor/executrix to take all steps necessary to carry out such arrangements.

IN WITNESS WHEREOF, I, **CATHY NAN SIMES,** testatrix, do hereby subscribe my name this the _____ day of _____ , 19___ , to this instrument and declare the same to be my Last Will and Testament, in the presence of _____ ,

_____

and_____

attesting witnesses at my request and in my presence and in the presence of each other.

_____

**TESTATRIX**

The foregoing instrument was now here published as the Last Will and Testament of **CATHY NAN SIMES,** and signed and subscribed by her, the Testatrix, in our presence, and we, at her request and in her presence and in the presence of each other signed and subscribed our names hereto as attesting witnesses.
Address:

_____    _____
                             Witness

_____
Address:

_____    _____
                             Witness

_____
Address:

_____    _____
                             Witness

_____

### (ADD SELF-PROVING AFFIDAVIT)

Model will for married person with children.

---

## LAST WILL AND TESTAMENT
## OF
## JOSEPH RALPH SMITH

STATE OF TEXAS
COUNTY OF HIDALGO
KNOW ALL MEN BY THESE PRESENTS:

THAT I, JOSEPH RALPH SMITH of HIDALGO County, Texas, and being of sound mind and disposing memory and above the age of eighteen (18) years, do make, publish and declare this my Last Will and Testament, hereby revoking all other wills and codicils heretofore made by me.

### I.

I declare that I am married to ROSIE JONNA SMITH, and that all references in this Will to my spouse are references to her. I have TWO children, now living, namely,

| EMERSON SMITH | FEB. 18, 1978 |
|---|---|
| | date of birth |
| BARBARA SMITH | OCT. 27, 1987 |
| | date of birth |

No other child or children, except as named above, were born to me at the date of execution of this Will and no child or children were adopted by me at the date of execution of this Will. All references in this Will to "my children" are to said named children and to any children hereafter born to or adopted by me.

### II.

I hereby appoint my spouse, ROSIE JONNA SMITH, as Independent Executrix of my Will and I direct that no bond shall be required of her. If for any reason she cannot, or refuses to act as Executrix, then I appoint GEORGE JAMES of DONNA, TEXAS, as Independent Executor of my Will, to serve without bond. If my spouse and GEORGE JAMES both fail or refuse to qualify, I appoint FIRST BANK OF DONNA as Independent Executor of my Will, to serve without bond. I direct that no action shall be had in any court in relation to the settlement of my estate other than the probating and recording of this Will and the return of a statutory inventory and appraisement and list of claims of my estate.

_____
TESTATOR

### III.

I give, devise, and bequeath to my beloved spouse, **ROSIE JON-NA SMITH**, all of my property, real, personal, and mixed and wheresoever located of every sort and description of which I may die possessed, or to which I may be entitled at the time of my death to have and to hold as her property absolutely.

### IV.

If my spouse, **ROSIE JONNA SMITH**, should predecease me, or if she and I die as a result of a common disaster or under such circumstances that there is not sufficient evidence to determine the order of our deaths, or if my spouse, **ROSIE JONNA SMITH**, shall die within a period of 30 days after the date of my death, then all bequests, devises, and provisions made herein to or for her bene- fit shall be void and my estate shall be administered and distributed in all respects as though my spouse, **ROSIE JONNA SMITH**, had not survived me.

### V.

If my spouse does not survive me, I direct that my entire estate go to my surviving children, **EMERSON SMITH** and **BARBARA SMITH** to share and share alike. If any child of mine is a minor at the time of my death, then I hereby deliver his/her estate to **GEORGE JAMES** as guardian of the estate of my child, **GEORGE JAMES**, to serve without bond. If for any reason **GEORGE JAMES** cannot act in such capacity, then I appoint **LEE EARL**, of **DONNA, TEXAS**, to act as guardian of the estate of my child and to serve without bond.

### VI.

In the event that at any time it may be necessary to appoint a guardian for the person of any child of mine, then I nominate and appoint as such guardian **GEORGE JAMES**, and if for any rea- son he shall fail or cease so to serve I nominate and appoint in his place **LEE EARL** as guardian hereunder, and I direct that no guardian shall be required to furnish any bond.

### VII.

In the event that any of my children shall predecease me or if he/she and I die as a result of a common disaster or under such cir- cumstances that there is not sufficient evidence to determine the order of

---

TESTATOR

our deaths, then all bequests, devises, and provisions made herein to or for his/her benefit shall be void and my estate shall be administered and distributed in all respects as though my child/children had not survived me.

### VIII.

In the event that none of the persons designated herein survive me, then I direct that my estate pass to my heirs at law.

### IX.

No one shall be deemed to have survived me unless that person survives at least 30 days after the date of my death.

IN WITNESS WHEREOF, I, JOSEPH RALPH SMITH, testator, do hereby subscribe my name this the 21st day of JUNE, 1994, to this instrument and declare the same to be my Last Will and Testament, in the presence of _____

_____ , _____
and_____
attesting witnesses at my request and in my presence and in the presence of each other.

_____
TESTATOR

The foregoing instrument was now here published as the Last Will and Testament of JOSEPH RALPH SMITH, and signed and subscribed by him, the Testator, in our presence, and we, at his request and in his presence and in the presence of each other signed and subscribed our names hereto as attesting witnesses.
Address:

_____    _____
                             Witness

_____
Address:

_____    _____
                             Witness

_____
Address:

_____    _____
                             Witness

_____

### (ADD SELF-PROVING AFFIDAVIT)

**The Self-Proving Affidavit should be added at the end of any will.**

---

### SELF-PROVING AFFIDAVIT
For Will

STATE OF TEXAS

COUNTY OF _____

Before me, the undersigned authority, on this day personally appeared _____ ,

_____ ,

_____

and _____ ,
known to me to be testator/testatrix and the witnesses, respectively, whose names are subscribed to the annexed or foregoing instrument in their respective capacities, and all of said persons being by me duly sworn, the said _____ , testator/testatrix, declared to me and to the said witnesses in my presence that said instrument is his/her last will and testament, and that he/she had willingly made and executed it as his/her free act and deed for the purposes therein expressed; and the said witnesses, each on their oath, stated to me, in the presence and hearing of the said testator/testatrix, that the said testator/testatrix had declared to them that said instrument is his/her last will and testament, and that he/she executed same as such and wanted each of them to sign as a witness; and upon their oaths each witness stated further that they did sign the same as witnesses in the presence of the said testator/testatrix and at his/her request; that he/she was at the time eighteen years of age or over and was of sound mind, and that each of said witnesses was then at least fourteen years of age.

_____

Testator/Testatrix

Address:

_____    _____

Witness

Address:

_____    _____

Witness

Address:

_____    _____

Witness

SUBSCRIBED AND ACKNOWLEDGED before me by the said testator/testatrix, —————————————————————————,
and subscribed and sworn to before me by the said  ——————————
——————————————— , ———————————————————
and  ————————————————————————————————,
witnesses, this ——— day of ——————, 19———.

—————————————————————
Notary Public

My commission expires:

—————————————————————

The Texas legislature's suggested form for a directive to physicians, or "living will."

## DIRECTIVE TO PHYSICIANS

Directive made this _____ day of _____ (month, year).

I, _____ , being of sound mind willfully and voluntarily make known my desire that my life shall not be artificially prolonged under the circumstances set forth below, and do hereby declare:

1. If at any time I should have an incurable or irreversible condition caused by injury, disease, or illness certified to be a terminal condition by two physicians, and where the application of life-sustaining procedures would serve only to artificially prolong the moment of my death and where my attending physician determines that my death is imminent or will result within a relatively short time without application of life-sustaining procedures, I direct that such procedures be withheld or withdrawn, and that I be permitted to die naturally.

2. In the absence of my ability to give directions regarding the use of such life-sustaining procedures, it is my intention that this directive shall be honored by my family and physicians as the final expression of my legal right to refuse medical or surgical treatment and accept the consequences from such refusal.

3. I understand that Texas law allows me to designate another person to make a treatment decision for me if I should become comatose, incompetent, or otherwise mentally or physically incapable of communication. I hereby designate _____ who resides at _____ to make such a treatment decision for me if I should become incapable of communicating with my physician. If the person I have named above is unable to act on my behalf, I authorize the following person to do so:

   Name: _____

   Address:_____

I have discussed my wishes with these persons and trust their judgment.

4. If I have been diagnosed as pregnant and that diagnosis is known to my physician, this directive shall have no force or effect during the course of my pregnancy.

5. This directive shall be in effect until it is revoked.

6. I understand the full import of this directive and I am emotionally and mentally competent to make this directive.

7. I understand that I may revoke this directive at any time.

Signed _____

City _____ County _____ , TEXAS

I am not related to the declarant by blood or marriage; nor would I be entitled to any portion of the declarant's estate on his/her decease; nor am I the attending physician of the declarant or an employee of the attending physician; nor am I a patient in the health care facility in which the declarant is a patient, or any person who has a claim against any portion of the estate of the declarant upon his/her decease. Furthermore, if I am an employee of a health facility in which the declarant is a patient, I am not involved in providing direct patient care to the declarant nor am I directly involved in the financial affairs of the health facility.

Witness _____ Witness _____

*May be removed from book by reader. Cut along dotted line.*

**The Statutory Durable Power of Attorney gives your designated agent the power to make decisions regarding your property and financial matters in the event that you are unable to do so.**

## STATUTORY DURABLE POWER OF ATTORNEY

NOTICE: THE POWERS GRANTED BY THIS DOCUMENT ARE BROAD AND SWEEPING. THEY ARE EXPLAINED IN THE DURABLE POWER OF ATTORNEY ACT, CHAPTER XII, TEXAS PROBATE CODE. IF YOU HAVE ANY QUESTIONS ABOUT THESE POWERS, OBTAIN COMPETENT LEGAL ADVICE. THIS DOCUMENT DOES NOT AUTHORIZE ANY-ONE TO MAKE MEDICAL AND OTHER HEALTH-CARE DECISIONS FOR YOU. YOU MAY REVOKE THIS POWER OF ATTORNEY IF YOU LATER WISH TO DO SO.

I, _____ (insert your name and address), my social security number being __ __ __ - __ __ - __ __ __ __ (insert your proper SS#), appoint _____ (insert the name and address of person appointed) as my agent (attorney-in-fact) to act for me in any lawful way with respect to the following initialed subjects:

TO GRANT ALL OF THE FOLLOWING POWERS, INITIAL THE LINE IN FRONT OF (N) AND IGNORE THE LINES IN FRONT OF THE OTHER POWERS.

TO GRANT ONE OR MORE, BUT FEWER THAN ALL, OF THE FOLLOWING POWERS, INITIAL THE LINE IN FRONT OF EACH POWER YOU ARE GRANTING.

TO WITHHOLD A POWER, DO NOT INITIAL THE LINE IN FRONT OF IT. YOU MAY, BUT NEED NOT, CROSS OUT EACH POWER WITHHELD.

INITIAL

_____ (A) real property transactions;

_____ (B) tangible personal property transactions;

_____ (C) stock and bond transactions;

_____ (D) commodity and option transactions;

_____ (E) banking and other financial institution transactions;

_____ (F) business operating transactions;

_____ (G) insurance and annuity transactions;

_____ (H) estate, trust, and other beneficiary transactions;

_____ (I) claims and litigation;

_____ (J) personal and family maintenance;

_____ (K) benefits from social security, Medicare, Medicaid, or other governmental programs or civil or military service;

_____ (L) retirement plan transactions;

_____ (M) tax matters;

_____ (N) ALL OF THE POWERS LISTED IN (A) THROUGH (M). YOU NEED NOT INITIAL ANY OTHER LINES IF YOU INITIAL LINE (N).

SPECIAL INSTRUCTIONS:

(IN THE FOLLOWING SPACE YOU MAY GIVE SPECIAL INSTRUCTIONS LIMITING OR EXTENDING THE POWERS GRANTED TO YOUR AGENT.)

_____

_____

_____

_____

_____

_____

UNLESS YOU DIRECT OTHERWISE ABOVE, THIS POWER OF ATTORNEY IS EFFECTIVE IMMEDIATELY AND WILL CONTINUE UNTIL IT IS REVOKED.

CHOOSE ONE OF THE FOLLOWING ALTERNATIVES BY CROSSING OUT THE ALTERNATIVE NOT CHOSEN:

(A) This power of attorney is not affected by my subsequent disability or incapacity.

(B) This power of attorney becomes effective upon my disability or incapacity.

YOU SHOULD CHOOSE ALTERNATIVE (A) IF THIS POWER OF ATTORNEY IS TO BECOME EFFECTIVE ON THE DATE IT IS EXECUTED.

_May be removed from book by reader. Cut along dotted line._

IF NEITHER (A) OR (B) IS CROSSED OUT, IT WILL BE ASSUMED THAT YOU CHOSE ALTERNATIVE (A).

I agree that any third party who receives a copy of this document may act under it. Revocation of the durable power of attorney is not effective as to a third party until the third party receives actual notice of the revocation. I agree to indemnify the third party for any claims that arise against the third party because of reliance on this power of attorney.

If any agent named by me dies, becomes legally disabled, resigns, or refuses to act, I name the following (each to act alone and successively, in the order named) as successor(s) to that agent:
_____ ,

Signed this _____ day of _____ , 19___ .

_____
(your signature)
State of _____
County of _____

This document was acknowledged before me on

_____ _____ (date) by

_____
(name of principal)

_____
(signature of notarial officer)

(Seal, if any, of
notary)_____
(printed name)

My commission expires: _____

THE ATTORNEY IN FACT OR AGENT, BY ACCEPTING OR ACTING UNDER THE APPOINTMENT, ASSUMES THE FIDUCIARY AND OTHER LEGAL RESPONSIBILITIES OF AN AGENT.

# INDEX